W9-AKC-635

# ENERGY

**THIRD EDITION**

Ferguson's
*An Infobase Learning Company*

Careers in Focus: Energy, Third Edition

Copyright ©2012 by Infobase Learning

Ferguson's
An imprint of Infobase Learning
132 West 31st Street
New York NY 10001

Library of Congress Cataloging-in-Publication Data

Careers in focus. Energy. — 3rd ed.
    p. cm. — (Careers in focus)
  Includes bibliographical references and index.
  ISBN-13: 978-0-8160-8039-7 (hardcover : alk. paper)
  ISBN-10: 0-8160-8039-9 (hardcover : alk. paper)  1. Energy industries—
Vocational guidance—Juvenile literature. I. Title: Energy.
  TJ163.2.C367 2011
  333.79023—dc23                              2011017822

Ferguson's books are available at special discounts when purchased in bulk quantities for businesses, associations, institutions, or sales promotions. Please call our Special Sales Department in New York at (212) 967-8800 or (800) 322-8755.

You can find Ferguson's on the World Wide Web at
http://www.infobaselearning.com

Text design by David Strelecky
Composition by Erika K. Arroyo
Cover printed by Yurchak Printing, Landisville, Pa.
Book printed and bound by Yurchak Printing, Landisville, Pa.
Date printed: October 2011
Printed in the United States of America

10 9 8 7 6 5 4 3 2 1

This book is printed on acid-free paper.

All links and Web addresses were checked and verified to be correct at the time of publication. Because of the dynamic nature of the Web, some addresses and links may have changed since publication and may no longer be valid.

# Table of Contents

# Introduction

*Careers in Focus: Energy* describes a variety of careers in the demanding, yet rewarding, world of energy—in laboratories, coal mines, deep-sea exploration rigs, nuclear power plants, petroleum refineries, electric power plants, and countless other settings. These careers are as diverse in nature as they are in their earnings and educational requirements.

Earnings range from less than $20,000 for clerical support workers to more than $186,000 for experienced nuclear engineers. A few of these careers—such as coal miners, energy conservation technicians, and power plant workers—require little formal education, but are excellent starting points for a career in the industry. Others—such as nuclear reactor operators—require some postsecondary training or the completion of an apprenticeship. The majority of jobs in the energy industry (such as geologists, nuclear engineers, and solar engineers), though, require a minimum of a bachelor's degree.

The outlook for energy jobs varies by industry. The *Career Guide to Industries* predicts that employment in utilities (including natural gas distribution and electric power generation, transmission, and distribution) will decline by 11 percent through 2018. Employment in the mining industry is expected to decline by 14 percent through 2018, and employment in the oil and gas extraction industry is expected to decline by 16 percent during the same time span. Despite these poor employment outlooks, job prospects for specific professions in these industries are expected to be good. The U.S. Department of Labor (DOL) predicts that employment opportunities will be favorable for geologists, geophysicists, mining engineers, petroleum engineers, and surveyors.

One energy sector that is experiencing steady growth is renewable energy, which is defined as a clean and unlimited source of power or fuel. This energy is harnessed from different sources such as wind, sunlight (solar), water (hydro), organic matter (biomass), and the earth's internal heat (geothermal). In 2009, renewable energy sources made up 8.2 percent of total U.S. energy consumption and 10.5 percent of electricity generation, according to the Energy Information Administration. Another area of growth is energy conservation. Individuals and businesses, schools, government agencies, and other organizations are seeking ways to reduce energy output and waste, which is creating demand for energy conservation professionals.

In 2005, Congress passed the Energy Policy Act in an attempt to create a national energy policy and assist the energy industry. The 10-year, $11.5 billion measure provides tax breaks to traditional and renewable energy producers, seeks to modernize our nation's energy infrastructure, and encourages energy conservation and efficiency. Although the act met with approval from some segments of the public and government, others countered that the act didn't go far enough to address skyrocketing gas prices and reduce our nation's dependence on foreign oil. They also felt that the act weakened the Clean Water Act and the Safe Drinking Act.

Despite these employment predictions and the controversy over the benefits of the act, there will always be a need for qualified workers in the energy field—especially those with advanced education and knowledge of the latest energy-related technologies.

Each article in this book discusses a particular energy occupation in detail. The articles in *Careers in Focus: Energy* appear in Ferguson's *Encyclopedia of Careers and Vocational Guidance,* but have been updated and revised with the latest information from the DOL, professional organizations, and other sources. The following paragraphs detail the sections and features that appear in the book.

The **Quick Facts** section provides a brief summary of the career, including recommended school subjects, personal skills, work environment, minimum educational requirements, salary ranges, certification or licensing requirements, and employment outlook. This section also provides acronyms and identification numbers for the following government classification indexes: the Dictionary of Occupational Titles (DOT), the Guide for Occupational Exploration (GOE), the National Occupational Classification (NOC) Index, and the Occupational Information Network (O*NET)-Standard Occupational Classification System (SOC) index. The DOT, GOE, and O*NET-SOC indexes have been created by the U.S. government; the NOC index is Canada's career classification system. Readers can use the identification numbers listed in the Quick Facts section to access further information about a career. Print editions of the DOT (*Dictionary of Occupational Titles*. Indianapolis, Ind.: JIST Works, 1991) and GOE (*Guide for Occupational Exploration*. Indianapolis, Ind.: JIST Works, 2001) are available at libraries. Electronic versions of the DOT (http://www.oalj.dol.gov/libdot.htm), NOC (http://www5.hrsdc.gc.ca/NOC), and O*NET-SOC (http://www.onetonline.org) are available on the Internet. When no DOT, GOE, NOC, or O*NET-SOC numbers are listed, this means that the U.S. Department of Labor or Human Resources and Skills Development Canada have not created a numerical designation for this career. In this instance, you will see the acronym "N/A," or not available.

The **Overview** section is a brief introductory description of the duties and responsibilities involved in this career. Oftentimes, a career may have a variety of job titles. When this is the case, alternative career titles are presented. Employment statistics are also provided, when available. The **History** section describes the history of the particular job as it relates to the overall development of its industry or field. The **Job** describes the primary and secondary duties of the job. **Requirements** discusses high school and postsecondary education and training requirements, any certification or licensing that is necessary, and other personal requirements for success in the job. **Exploring** offers suggestions on how to gain experience in or knowledge of the particular job before making a firm educational and financial commitment. The focus is on what can be done while still in high school (or in the early years of college) to gain a better understanding of the job. The **Employers** section gives an overview of typical places of employment for the job. **Starting Out** discusses the best ways to land that first job, be it through the college career services office, newspaper ads, Internet employment sites, or personal contact. The **Advancement** section describes what kind of career path to expect from the job and how to get there. **Earnings** lists salary ranges and describes the typical fringe benefits. The **Work Environment** section describes the typical surroundings and conditions of employment—whether indoors or outdoors, noisy or quiet, social or independent. Also discussed are typical hours worked, any seasonal fluctuations, and the stresses and strains of the job. The **Outlook** section summarizes the job in terms of the general economy and industry projections. For the most part, Outlook information is obtained from the U.S. Bureau of Labor Statistics and is supplemented by information gathered from professional associations. Job growth terms follow those used in the *Occupational Outlook Handbook*. Growth described as "much faster than the average" means an increase of 20 percent or more. Growth described as "faster than the average" means an increase of 14 to 19 percent. Growth described as "about as fast as the average" means an increase of 7 to 13 percent. Growth described as "more slowly than the average" means an increase of 3 to 6 percent. "Little or no change" means a decrease of 2 percent to an increase of 2 percent. "Decline" means a decrease of 3 percent or more. Each article ends with **For More Information,** which lists organizations that provide information on training, education, internships, scholarships, and job placement.

*Careers in Focus: Energy* also includes photos, informative sidebars, and interviews with professionals in the field.

# Bioenergy/Biofuels Workers

## QUICK FACTS

**School Subjects**
Biology
Chemistry
Mathematics
Technical/shop

**Personal Skills**
Communication/ideas
Helping/teaching
Technical/scientific

**Work Environment**
Indoors and outdoors
Primarily multiple locations

**Minimum Education Level**
Varies by specialty

**Salary Range**
$18,430 to $56,270 to
$151,630+

**Certification or Licensing**
Required for certain
positions

**Outlook**
Faster than the average

**DOT**
003, 005, 007, 008, 010, 012,
013, 019, 024, 040, 041

**GOE**
02.03.02, 02.03.03,
02.07.01, 02.07.04,
02.08.04, 06.01.01

**NOC**
2121, 2131, 2132, 2133,
2134, 2148, 2211, 2231,
2232

*(continues)*

## OVERVIEW

Energy that is derived from biomass (organic material such as wood, plants, or animal wastes) is known as *bioenergy*. Bioenergy can be used to generate electricity and produce heat. It can also be used to produce *biofuels*, which are used in place of fossil fuels to power vehicles and for small heating applications. A wide range of jobs are available in the bioenergy and biofuels industry for people with various backgrounds and interests, including scientists, biologists, researchers and research technicians, plant managers, product managers, and sales engineers.

## HISTORY

Renewable energy sources have been around for thousands of years. Wood, corn, soy, aquatic plants, and animal waste are a small sampling of the types of organic, replenishable materials that can be converted into fuels to power cars and trucks, and provide heat and electricity to homes and buildings. In fact, wood is one of the earliest biofuels—cavemen were the first to figure out how to use it to improve their quality of life. With fire, food was cooked and hot, homes were warm, and nights were brighter. Vegetable oil is another early biofuel. In 1890, Rudolf Diesel, the inventor of the diesel-fueled engine (as you may have guessed), demonstrated his engine at the World Exhibition in Paris, France, by using peanut oil to power it. Ford's Model T, which

4

was produced from 1903–1926, was designed to run on hemp-derived bio-fuel. Back then, the abundance (not to mention the lower price and better efficiency) of fossil fuels pushed interest in biofuels to the wayside. Petroleum, among others, became the star.

As history has proven, one side effect of fuel shortages and energy crises is usually renewed interest in alternative energy sources. When faced with acute fuel shortages during World War II, Germany turned to potato-derived ethanol and wood-derived methanol as sources of fuel. The fuel crisis in the 1970s highlighted America's dependence on foreign-imported oil and the need to explore other sources of energy.

| QUICK FACTS |
| --- |
| *(continued)* |
| **O\*NET-SOC** |
| 11-3051.03, 11-3051.04, 11-9041.01, 17-2021.00, 17-2041.00, 17-2051.00, 17-2071.00, 17-2072.00, 17-2081.00, 17-2141.00, 17-2199.99, 17-3022.00, 17-3023.00, 17-3025.00, 17-3026.00, 17-3027.00, 17-3029.99, 19-1013.01, 19-1029.00, 19-2041.00, 19-4011.01, 19-4021.00, 19-4091.00, 47-1011.01 |

America's consumption of foreign oil was at a high by the early 1970s, while production of oil on U.S. lands was at an all-time low. The fuel crisis started in 1973, when Middle Eastern countries, to illustrate their anger over outsiders' involvement in Arab-Israeli conflicts, placed an embargo (meaning a legal stoppage) on petroleum exports to Western Nations, including the United Stated and the Netherlands. As a result, awareness of natural resources and energy conservation grew. More people started buying smaller, fuel-efficient cars, as opposed to the gas-guzzlers that had once been popular. Carpooling and mass transit were heavily promoted as ways to save energy and money. And interest in and funding for bioenergy and biofuels research grew.

## THE JOB

Bioenergy can be derived from wood, construction and consumer waste, landfill gas, and liquid biofuels such as ethanol for use in generating electricity, producing heat, and fueling vehicles. The United States gets approximately 4 percent of its energy from bioenergy, including wood and crops such as corn and soybeans.

There are a variety of jobs in the bioenergy and biofuels industry, from scientists and researchers to engineers, construction workers, product and plant managers, and a whole host of others. People are needed to create and improve the products and the technology, oversee and manage the operations and staff, as well as to build the facilities in which the work is done.

## Types of Biomass

- Agricultural Crops (cornstarch and corn oil, wheat starch, soybean oil and meal, and vegetable oils)
- Agriculture Crop Residues (stalks and leaves that are not harvested with crops)
- Animal Waste (from farms and animal-processing operations)
- Aquatic Crops (algae, giant kelp, other seaweed, and marine microflora)
- Biomass Processing Residues (unused sawdust, branches, bark, and leaves/needles)
- Dedicated Energy Crops (grasses, fast-growing hardwood trees)
- Forestry Residues (biomass not removed or harvested from logging sites or dead or dying trees)
- Municipal Waste (cardboard, waste paper, wood waste, and yard waste)

Source: U.S. Department of Energy

*Scientists* and *biologists* may work in the areas of research and development, to help advance the ways in which bioenergy and biofuels are produced. For instance, a *bioenergy plant scientist* may be involved in bioenergy crop research, conducting studies on plant growth and development, and plant adaptation to environmental stresses. This scientist's work may involve molecular studies of plants, in an effort to understand gene compositions and functions. A *seed production scientist* helps organize and manage seed production programs for companies. As described in one Internet advertisement for employment with a biofuels company in the agribusiness sector, the job can entail researching and developing seed production techniques for bioenergy grass crops, and include selecting production sites, field design, seed crop establishment, flowering and pollination control, seed harvest and handling, and developing quality-control programs.

*Biological technicians* work closely with biologists to research and study living organisms. They work as laboratory assistants, helping to set up, operate, and maintain laboratory equipment. They also monitor experiments, make observations, calculate and record results, and develop research conclusions. They may work in biotechnology, conducting basic research on gene splicing and recombinant DNA and applying knowledge and techniques to product development for biofuels and bioenergy. *Agricultural technicians* have similar roles in providing laboratory and research assistance, with their subject matter being crop production and processes. They conduct tests and experiments to improve the yield and quality of crops, and to help increase plants' resistance to disease, insects, or other hazards.

A *biofuels product manager* will work closely with business development managers, business analysts, and other product managers to help strategize business plans, product development, and product launches of biofuels. One posting for an ethanol product manager included job responsibilities such as interpreting customer and market needs and translating this information to research and development groups. Problem-solving abilities, strong communication skills, and the knack for analyzing data and communicating and presenting it clearly to different groups of people are required to succeed as a product manager. Other requirements may include guiding and participating in conferences, helping to create product strategies (including functionality, pricing, etc.), product application development and prototype testing, and handling communications with external groups.

*Biofuels plant managers* oversee all operations of biofuels and biorefinery plants, and are responsible for everything from machinery functionality to staff performance. A posting for a biofuels plant manager in Minnesota included the following job responsibilities:

- Ensure production is efficient and maximized.

- Provide direction to ensure proper levels of maintenance as well as compliance with safety and environmental regulations.

- Direct continuous improvements and quality-assurance efforts.

- Lead cross-functional efforts to facilitate best practices and process initiatives.

- Provide solid leadership; serve as a role model for the plant's management team.

- Revise policies and procedures as necessary to achieve the highest levels of morale and working relationships.

- Prepare and manage plant-wide budgets.

Candidates applying for this job also needed to have strong knowledge of chemical distillation, fermentation, and grain refining, processing, and extracting processes. They also needed prior experience in a petroleum, ethanol, biodiesel, biofuels, or chemical plant.

*Engineers* and *construction managers and workers* are also needed to create bioenergy and biofuels plants. *Civil, electrical, industrial,* and *mechanical engineers* develop designs for plants and process equipment using computer-aided design and computer-aided industrial design software. They work closely with architects, developers, business owners, construction crews, and others to make sure the work is done according to specifications. Construction managers coordinate the construction process, selecting and managing construction workers, and overseeing projects from the development phase to final construction. They may work as project manager, site manager, construction superintendent, project engineer, program manager, or general contractor.

## REQUIREMENTS

### High School
Course work in math, science, physics, history, English, and computer software programs will provide a well-rounded basis for this career. Foreign language classes are also useful. If your school offers environmental studies classes, take these as well. Some bioenergy and biofuels jobs may require knowledge of machines, so it may be advantageous to take electronics, mechanics, and shop classes.

### Postsecondary Training
Undergraduate requirements will vary depending on the job. Many companies and universities prefer to hire scientists, biologists, and researchers that have a bachelor's degree in science, and a Ph.D. in their specialty, which could be plant biology, biochemistry, physiology or genetics, to name only a few. Previous related research and project work may also be required for more advanced positions. Engineers may have a bachelor's or advanced degree in electrical, electronics, industrial, mechanical, or even civil engineering. Plant managers and product managers may have a bachelor's degree in business administration, management, industrial technology, or industrial engineering. Some jobs require a master's or Ph.D. in business, marketing, chemistry, biotechnology, or related fields, with experience in the biofuels industry. Some companies may hire plant or product managers with a liberal arts degree who match all other requirements of the job and can be trained while on the job.

## Certification or Licensing

Certification or licensing may be required for certain positions in the field. Contact your state's department of licensing for more information on requirements in your state. Engineering is one profession that is strongly regulated. Most states require engineers to be licensed. There are two levels of licensing for engineers. Professional engineers (PEs) have graduated from an accredited engineering curriculum, have four years of engineering experience, and have passed a written exam. Engineering graduates need not wait until they have four years experience, however, to start the licensure process. Those who pass the Fundamentals of Engineering examination after graduating are called engineers in training (EIT) or engineer interns (EI). The EIT certification usually is valid for 10 years. After acquiring suitable work experience, EITs can take the second examination, the Principles and Practice of Engineering exam, to gain full PE licensure.

## Other Requirements

Most bioenergy and biofuels jobs require strong oral and written communication skills to write reports, present materials, and manage staff. Scientists, researchers, and engineers usually work on teams, so the ability to share information and deal with different people is essential to succeeding in this type of work. Some positions may require knowledge of computer modeling, digital mapping, global positioning systems (GPS), and geographic information systems (GIS). Plant managers and product managers need strong organization skills in their work, as well as leadership and management abilities. Engineers will need to be well-versed in computer-aided design (CAD) and computer-aided industrial design (CAID) software systems. Knowledge of foreign languages can also be extremely beneficial in this field.

# EXPLORING

Keep up with developments and trends in bioenergy and biofuels by reading magazines and books. Pick an area of bioenergy and biofuels that interests you, then do an Internet search to find the companies that specialize in this area. If any are located near you, see if they have part time or summer job openings or volunteer opportunities. You can also find resources, event listings, and job postings on the *Biofuels Digest* Web site (http://biofuelsdigest.com). The site also features a useful article called "The Hottest 50 Companies in Bioenergy (2010–2011)," with direct links to each of the companies.

Internships, part-time jobs, and volunteer gigs are great ways to explore the bioenergy and biofuels field and see if this type of work suits you. Visit the Web sites of professional associations in the areas that interest you and see if there are opportunities to volunteer and get involved. Some resources are listed at the end of this profile to help you start exploring the field.

## EMPLOYERS

Scientists, biologists, and researchers work for universities, laboratories, and research institutes, as well as government agencies and private firms. According to the U.S. Department of Labor (DOL), there are about 85,900 environmental scientists employed in the United States. About 37 percent of all environmental scientists work for state and local governments. Another 21 percent work for management, scientific, and technical consulting services; and 15 percent work for architectural, engineering, and related services. About 7 percent work in the federal government.

The DOL reports that about 91,300 biological scientists are employed in the United States. (This number does not include the many who hold biology faculty positions in colleges and universities, as these are categorized as postsecondary teaching jobs.) Federal, state, and local governments employ about 40 percent of all biological scientists. The U.S. Departments of Agriculture, Interior, and Defense and the National Institutes of Health are the main employers of federal biological scientists. The remainder work in scientific research and testing laboratories, the pharmaceutical and medicine manufacturing industry, or colleges and universities.

Agricultural scientists hold about 31,000 positions. They work for federal, state, and local agencies; agricultural service companies; commercial research and development laboratories, seed companies; wholesale distributors; and food products companies. About 12 percent are self-employed as consultants.

Science technicians (including agricultural and biological technicians) hold about 270,800 jobs. Government agencies and scientific and technical service firms are their main employers.

Engineers hold approximately 1.6 million jobs in the United States. About 36 percent work in manufacturing industries, and 30 percent are employed in the professional, scientific, and technical services sector. And of the 156,100 industrial production managers employed in the United States, about 80 percent work in manufacturing industries.

## STARTING OUT

Many bioenergy/biofuels obtain their first jobs in the field as a result of contacts made through internships, volunteerships, or part-time positions. Others learn about job openings via career fairs, networking events, and the services of their college's career services office. You can also find useful information about careers in the renewable and clean energy industry by visiting the U.S. Department of Energy's Clean Energy Jobs section at http://www1.eere.energy.gov/education/clean_energy_jobs.html.

## ADVANCEMENT

Scientists and biologists can advance to more senior-management positions, such as department directors or regional supervisors. Plant and product managers with years of experience and proven track records can advance to regional manager, vice president, or a similar position of higher authority. Some workers may decide to freelance as consultants or start their own companies. Others can advance by teaching in colleges and universities, speaking at conferences held by industry associations, and writing papers and books on their area of specialty. Obtaining certification may not be required for some positions, but it can be attractive to prospective employers as it demonstrates knowledge in that subject. Getting a master's degree or Ph.D. can also help boost a candidate's chances for employment in certain areas of the bioenergy and biofuels field.

## EARNINGS

According to the DOL, in 2009 environmental scientists had median annual incomes of $61,010, with the lowest paid 10 percent earning less than $37,120 and the top paid 10 percent earning $107,190 or more.

Biological scientists' salaries in 2009 ranged from less than $36,750 to $100,580 or more. Annual salaries for soil and plant scientists in 2009 ranged from less than $34,930 to $107,670 or more. Biological technicians had median incomes of $38,700, with salaries ranging from less than $24,540 to $61,380 or more. Agricultural technicians earned less than $22,100 to $55,190 or more per year.

Industrial production managers earned median annual incomes of $85,080 in 2009, with the bottom 10 percent bringing home $51,290 or less, and the top 10 percent earning $146,030 or more. In 2009, construction managers had annual salaries ranging from less than

$49,320 to $151,630 or more, with median incomes of $82,330. Construction laborers' salaries ranged from less than $18,430 for the bottom 10 percent, to $56,270 or higher for the top 10 percent.

Engineers' salaries varied, depending on their specialty. For example, in 2009 environmental engineers earned annual incomes ranging from less than $47,660 to $115,750 or more; agricultural engineers brought home less than $42,980 to $116,240 or more each year; and chemical engineers earned less than $56,090 to $132,980 or more annually.

Bioenergy/biofuels workers who are employed full time receive benefits such as vacation days, sick leave, health and life insurance, and a savings and pension program. Self-employed workers must provide their own benefits.

## WORK ENVIRONMENT

Scientists, biologists, and research associates and technicians work indoors in laboratories and offices. They may spend some time outdoors conducting research on plants and crops and collecting samples. Engineers may also work in laboratories and offices, as well as outdoors, depending on the project. Construction managers and workers work on-site at construction sites and in offices. Product and plant managers work indoors in manufacturing facilities and plants, as well as in offices.

Work hours will vary, but most bioenergy and biofuels positions will require at least 40-hour workweeks, with additional hours occasionally needed on evenings and weekends to meet project deadlines. Some positions will require travel for research, meetings, and conferences.

## OUTLOOK

The U.S. economic stimulus plan included $500 million for "leading-edge" biofuels projects. With the government's interest in funding bioenergy and biofuels research and increasing the supply of biofuels, environmental science and research jobs in this field are expected to be on the rise in the years to come.

The DOL predicts that employment for environmental scientists will grow much faster than average for all careers through 2018, with private sector consulting firms offering the most job opportunities. Stricter environmental laws and regulations will increase the need for scientists and researchers working in the bioenergy and biofuels arena.

Biological scientists will also have strong employment opportunities through 2018 because of the focus on cleaning up the environment and reducing carbon and greenhouse gas emissions. According to the DOL, demand for biological scientists will continue to grow due to the need to study the impact of industry and government actions on the environment, and develop ways to prevent and correct environmental problems. Environmental regulatory agencies will need biological scientists to help advise lawmakers and lawyers on environmental legislation. The need for alternative fuel will also increase the demand for biological scientists who specialize in biotechnology (e.g., using ethanol for transportation fuel).

Employment for agricultural engineers is expected to grow about as fast as the average for all occupations through 2018. They will be needed to research and develop biofuels and biotechnology, and to create more efficient crops dedicated to biofuels production and renewable energy sources. Construction managers are also expected to have good job opportunities through 2018, according to the DOL. Those with bachelor's degrees, or higher, in construction science, construction management, or civil engineering, along with practical, related work experience will have the advantage in the job market.

## FOR MORE INFORMATION

### Agricultural Sciences
*To learn more about agricultural science careers, visit*
American Society of Agronomy
Crop Science Society of America
Soil Science Society of America
5585 Guilford Road
Madison, WI 53711-5801
Tel: 608-273-8080
https://www.agronomy.org
https://www.crops.org/
https://www.soils.org/

### Biological Sciences
*For publications, networking opportunities, policy information, and other information related to the biological sciences, visit*
American Institute of Biological Sciences
1444 I Street, NW, Suite 200
Washington, DC 20005-6535
Tel: 202-628-1500
http://www.aibs.org

## Chemical Sciences

*For chemical scientist and chemical technician information, visit*
American Chemical Society
1155 16th Street, NW
Washington, DC 20046-4839
Tel: 800-227-5558
E-mail: help@acs.org
http://www.acs.org

## Construction

*For more information about construction careers, visit*
American Institute of Constructors & Constructor
   Certification Commission
700 North Fairfax Street, Suite 510
Alexandria, VA 22314-2090
Tel: 703-683-4999
http://www.professionalconstructor.org

## Engineering

*For more information about engineering schools and career resources, visit the society's Web site.*
American Society for Engineering Education
1818 N Street, NW, Suite 600
Washington, DC 20036-2479
Tel: 202-331-3500
http://www.asee.org

*Find out more about engineering careers by visiting*
Junior Engineering Technical Society
1420 King Street, Suite 405
Alexandria, VA 22314-2750
Tel: 703-548-5387
http://www.jets.org

## General Energy and Bioenergy Information

*Learn more about energy issues and find out about upcoming events and conferences by visiting*
American Council for an Energy-Efficient Economy
529 14th Street, NW, Suite 600
Washington, DC 20045-1000
Tel: 202-507-4000
http://www.aceee.org

*For industry news and updates and general information on bioenergy, contact*

Renewable Fuels Association
425 Third Street, SW, Suite 1150
Washington, DC 20024-3231
Tel: 202-289-3835
http://www.ethanolrfa.org

*Learn more about bioenergy and bioenergy programs by visiting*

U.S. Department of Energy
1000 Independence Avenue, SW
Washington, DC 20585-0001
Tel: 202-586-5000
http://www.energy.gov/energysources/bioenergy.htm

## Product and Plant Management

*To learn more about industrial production management careers, contact*

Association for Operations Management
8430 West Bryn Mawr Avenue, Suite 1000
Chicago, IL 60631-3417
Tel: 800-444-2742
http://www.apics.org

# Coal Miners

## QUICK FACTS

**School Subjects**
Chemistry
Earth science

**Personal Skills**
Mechanical/manipulative
Technical/scientific

**Work Environment**
Indoors and outdoors
Primarily one location

**Minimum Education Level**
High school diploma

**Salary Range**
$28,750 to $43,010 to
$62,110+

**Certification or Licensing**
Required by certain states

**Outlook**
Decline

**DOT**
930

**GOE**
06.03.01

**NOC**
8231

**O*NET-SOC**
19-4041.00, 47-5041.00,
47-5042.00

## OVERVIEW

*Coal miners* extract coal from surface mines and underground mines. To do this, they operate complex and expensive machinery that drills, cuts, scrapes, or shovels earth and coal so that the fuel can be collected. Since coal is hard to reach, large portions of earth must be removed from the surface or dug out of mines so the coal miners can get to it. Some coal miners are explosives experts who use dynamite and other substances to remove earth and make the coal accessible. There are approximately 80,600 coal-mining workers employed in the United States.

## HISTORY

Even before the development of agriculture and weaving, Stone Age people mined minerals buried in the earth: flints for weaponry, mineral pigments for picture and body painting, and precious metals and stones for ornamentation. Early miners carved out open pits to reach the more accessible materials. Then they dug primitive tunnels underground, using sticks and bones to remove soft or broken rocks. As time went on, early miners learned to break hard rocks by driving metal or wooden wedges into cracks in the surface. An early method for dealing with particularly large, stubborn rocks was to build fires alongside them until they became thoroughly heated and then to dash cold water against them. The sudden contraction would cause the rocks to fracture.

No one knows when coal was first discovered and used for fuel; ancient peoples in several areas of the globe seem to have known about it. There is evidence that coal was burned in Wales during the Bronze Age about 4,000 years ago, and by the early Romans in Britain. The first industrial use of coal was in the Middle Ages in England; the English were far more advanced in mining methods than other nations for many years.

The earliest method of coal production was strip mining, which involves gathering deposits near the earth's surface. Early strip mining did not produce large amounts of coal because methods of removing soil that lay over the coal were crude and slow. Beginning in 1910, this type of mining became more practical as powered machinery came into use.

Commercial mining started in the United States around 1750, near Richmond, Virginia, with the first recorded commercial shipment of American coal: 32 tons from Virginia to New York. Most of the coal produced was used to manufacture shells and shot for the Revolutionary War.

The coal industry played a vital role in the rapid industrial development of the United States. Its importance increased dramatically during the 1870s, as the railroads expanded and the steel industry developed, and during the 1880s, when steam was first used to generate electric power. The production of bituminous coal doubled each decade from 1880 to 1910, and by 1919 production was more than 500 million tons.

Coal is the country's primary source of energy. Its use declined after World War II, when natural gas and oil became economically competitive, but rising petroleum prices and worries about the availability of oil have made coal a major energy source again. Coal production in the United States reached 1 billion tons for the first time in 1990. Today about half of the nation's electricity is generated by burning coal.

Modern technology and improved management have revolutionized coal mining in the last century. Specialized machinery has been developed that replaces human effort with electric, pneumatic, hydraulic, and mechanical power, which are remotely controlled in some applications by computers. This means that highly skilled technicians and workers are needed to direct, operate, maintain, modify, and control the work performed by very expensive machinery. However, with the growth of the coal-mining industry has come concern about the environmental impact of mining and burning coal.

## THE JOB

Coal miners work in two kinds of coal mines: surface and underground. The mining method used is determined by the depth and location of the coal seam and the geological formations around it. In surface or strip mining, the overburden—the earth above the coal seam—has to be removed before the coal can be dug out. Then, after the mining has been completed, the overburden is replaced so the land can be reclaimed. For underground mining, entries and tunnels are constructed so that workers and equipment can reach the coal.

The machinery used in coal mining is extremely complex and expensive. There are power shovels that can move 3,500 tons of earth in an hour and continuous mining machines that can rip 12 tons of coal from an underground seam in a minute. Longwall shearers can extract the coal at an even faster rate. The job of coal miners is to operate these machines safely and efficiently. Their specific duties depend on the type of mine in which they work and the machinery they operate. The following paragraphs provide more information about major specialties in the field.

*Drillers* operate drilling machines to bore holes in the overburden at points selected by the blasters. They must be careful that the drill doesn't bind or stop while in operation. They may replace worn or broken drill parts using hand tools, change drill bits, and lubricate the equipment.

## Fun Facts About Coal

- The first coal mining operations opened in Virginia in the mid-1700s.
- The United States produces approximately 35 percent of the world's coal. It ranks second in the world (after China) in coal production.
- Coal is found in 38 states.
- Wyoming is the top coal-producing state in the United States.
- Coal is used to generate about 50 percent of our nation's electricity.
- Coal is also used to create chemicals, cement, paper, ceramics, and metal products.
- Ash from coal is used in the production of golf balls, tennis rackets, and linoleum.
- Experts predict that the United States has a 245-year supply of coal if we continue our consumption at current rates.

Source: American Coal Foundation

*Stripping shovel operators* and *dragline operators* control the shovels and draglines that scoop up and move the broken overburden, which is pushed within their reach by the bulldozers. With the overburden removed, the coal is exposed so that machines with smaller shovels can remove it from the seam and load it into trucks.

Underground mining uses three methods to extract the coal that lies deep beneath the surface. These methods are continuous, longwall, and conventional mining.

Continuous mining is the most widely used method of mining underground coal. It is a system that uses a hydraulically operated machine that mines and loads coal in one step. Cutting wheels attached to hydraulic lifts rip coal from the seam. Then mechanical arms gather the coal from the tunnel floor and dump it onto a conveyor belt, which moves the coal to a shuttle car or another conveyor belt to be carried out of the mine. *Continuous-mining machine operators* sit or lie in the cab of the machine or operate it remotely. Either way, they move the machine into the mining area and manipulate levers to position the cutting wheels against the coal. These operators and their assistants may adjust, repair, and lubricate the machine and change cutting teeth.

In longwall mining, coal is also cut and loaded in one operation. With steel canopies supporting the roof above the work area, the mining machinery moves along a wall while its plow blade or cutting wheel shears the coal from the seam and automatically loads it onto a conveyor belt for transportation out of the mine. *Longwall-mining machine operators* advance the cutting device either manually or by remote control. They monitor lights and gauges on the control panel and listen for unusual sounds that would signal or indicate a malfunction in the equipment. As the wall in front of the longwall mining machine is cut away, the operator and face personnel move the roof supports forward, allowing the roof behind the supports to cave in.

Conventional mining, unlike continuous or longwall mining, is done in separate steps: first the coal is blasted from the seam, and then it is picked up and loaded. Of the three underground methods, conventional mining requires the largest number of workers. *Cutter operators* work a self-propelled machine equipped with a circular, toothed chain that travels around a blade six to 15 feet long. They drive the machine into the working area and saw a channel along the bottom and sides of the coalface, a procedure that makes the blasting more effective because it relieves some of the pressure caused by the explosion. Cutter operators may also adjust and repair the machine, replace dull teeth, and shovel debris from the channel. Using mobile machines, *drilling-machine operators* bore blast holes in the coalface after first determining the depth of the undercut and where to place the holes. Then *blasters* place explosive charges in the holes and detonate them to shatter the coal. After the blast, *loading-machine operators* drive electric loading machines to the area and manipulate the levers that control the mechanical arms to gather up the loose coal and load it onto shuttle cars or conveyors to be carried out of the mine.

*Coal mining technicians* play an important role in the mining process. By the time the mining actually starts, coal mining technicians have already helped the managers, engineers, and scientists to survey, test drill, and analyze the coal deposit for depth and quality. They have mapped the surface and helped plan the drilling and blasting to break up the rock and soil that cover the coal. The technicians have also helped prepare permits that must be filed with federal and state governments before mining can begin. Information must be provided on how the land will be mined and reclaimed; its soil, water conditions, and vegetation; wildlife conservation; and how archaeological resources will be protected.

Coal mining technicians also help the mining engineers and superintendents select the machinery used in mining. Such a plan must include selecting machines of a correct size and capacity to match other machinery and planning the sequences for efficient use of machines. They also assist in mapping roads out of the mine pit, planning machine and road maintenance and, above all, using safety methods for the entire operation.

*Ventilation technicians* operate dust counting, gas quantity, and air volume measuring instruments. They record or plot this data and plan or assist in planning the direction of airflow through mine workings. Ventilation technicians also help prescribe the fan installations required to accomplish the desired airflow.

*Geological aides* gather geological data as mining activities progress. They identify rocks and minerals; record and map structural changes; locate drill holes; and identify rocks, coal, and minerals in drill cores. They also map geological information from drill core data, gather samples, and map results on mine plans.

*Chemical analysts* analyze mine, mill, and coal samples by using volumetric or instrumental methods of analysis. They also write reports on the findings.

Mining work is hard, dirty, and often dangerous. Mine workers are often characterized by the concern they have for their fellow miners. There is no room for carelessness in this occupation. The safety of all workers depends on teamwork, with everyone alert and careful to avoid accidents.

# REQUIREMENTS

## High School

A high school diploma is a minimum educational requirement for this work. Coal miners must be at least 18 years of age and in good physical condition to withstand the rigors of the job.

To work in this field, you should complete at least two years of mathematics, including algebra and geometry, and four years of English and language skills courses, with emphasis on reading, writing, and communication training.

You should also take physics and chemistry. Computer skills are also important, particularly knowledge of computer-aided drafting and design programs. Courses in mechanical drawing or drafting are also helpful.

## Postsecondary Training

Federal laws require that all mine workers be given safety and health training before starting work and be retrained annually thereafter. Federal and state laws also require preservice training and annual retraining in subjects such as health and safety regulations and first aid.

It is possible to start a coal-mining career as an unskilled worker with a high school diploma, but it is difficult to advance within the coal mining industry without the foundation skills. In general, companies prefer employees who bring formally acquired technical knowledge and skills to the job.

The first year of study in a typical two-year coal mining technician program in a technical or community college includes courses in the basics of coal mining, applied mathematics, mining law, coal mining ventilation and atmospheric control, communication skills, technical reporting, fundamentals of electricity, mining machinery, physical geology, surveying and graphics, mine safety and accident prevention, roof and rib control, and industrial economics and financing.

The second year includes courses in mine instrumentation and electrical systems, electrical maintenance, hydraulic machinery, machine transmissions and drive trains, basic welding, coal mine environmental impacts and control, coal and coal mine atmosphere sampling and analysis, mine machinery and systems automation and control, application of computers to coal mining operations, and first aid and mine rescue.

In some programs, students spend the summer working as interns at coal mining companies. Internships provide a clear picture of the field and help you choose the work area that best fits your abilities.

You will gain experience using charts, graphs, blueprints, maps, and machinery and develop confidence through an approach to the real operation of the industry.

### Certification or Licensing

Requirements for certification of mine workers vary. A state may require that any person engaged at the face of the mine first obtain a certificate of competency as a miner from the state's miner's examining board. In some cases, a miner may obtain a certificate of competency after completing one year of underground work. A miner who has an associate's degree in coal mine technology may be able to obtain the certificate after completing six months of underground work.

For those seeking a certificate of competency as a mine examiner or manager, a state may require at least four years of underground experience; graduates with associate's degrees in coal mining technology, however, may be able to qualify after only three years of experience.

Coal mining technician students can usually meet the state's criteria for employment while still in their technician preparatory program. It is important to be familiar with these criteria if technicians plan to work in a state other than the one where they begin their education and work experience.

### Other Requirements

To be a successful coal miner, you will need to work well with others and accept supervision. You must also learn to work independently and accept responsibility. You must be accurate and careful, as mistakes can be expensive, hazardous, and even fatal.

## EXPLORING

Because of the age limitation for coal miners, opportunities do not exist for most high school students to gain actual experience. If you are over the age of 18, you may be able to find summer work as a laborer in a coal mine, performing routine tasks that require no previous experience. Older students may also investigate the possibility of summer or part-time employment in metal mines, quarries, oil drilling operations, heavy construction, road building, or truck driving. While this work may not be directly related to your career goals, the aptitudes required for the jobs are similar to those needed in mining, and the experience may prove useful.

# EMPLOYERS

There are approximately 80,600 coal-mining workers employed in the United States. Most coal miners work in private industry for mining companies. Some opportunities also exist with federal and state governments. Coal mining operations exist in 26 states, but the U.S. Department of Labor (DOL) notes that approximately 67 percent of coal-mining jobs are found in Kentucky, Pennsylvania, and West Virginia. Other states that employ a large number of coal miners include Alabama, Illinois, Indiana, Virginia, and Wyoming.

# STARTING OUT

The usual method of entering this field is by direct application to the employment offices of the individual coal mining companies. However, mining machine operators must "come up through the ranks," acquiring the necessary skills on the job.

New employees start as trainees, or red hats. After the initial training period, they work at routine tasks that do not require much skill, such as shoveling coal onto conveyors. As they gain more experience and become familiar with the mining operations, they are put to work as helpers to experienced machine operators. In this way they eventually learn how to operate the machines themselves.

Coal mining technicians are usually hired by recruiters from major employers before completing their last year of technical school. Industry recruiters regularly visit the campuses of schools with coal mining technician programs and work with the schools' placement officers.

Many two-year graduates take jobs emphasizing basic operational functions. Technicians are then in a position to compete for higher positions, in most cases through the system of job bidding, which considers such factors as formal education, experience, and seniority.

The union to which most unionized coal miners belong is the United Mine Workers of America, although some are covered by the International Union of Operating Engineers. Some independent unions also operate within single firms. These unions help their members find available jobs as well as support them once they are employed.

In union mines, when a vacancy occurs and a machine operator job is available, an announcement is posted so that any qualified employee can apply for the position. In most cases the job is given to the person with the most seniority.

## ADVANCEMENT

Advancement opportunities for coal miners are limited. The usual progression is from trainee to general laborer to machine operator's helper. After acquiring the skills needed to operate the machinery, helpers may apply for machine operator jobs as they become available. All qualified workers, however, compete for those positions, and vacancies are almost always filled by workers with the most seniority. A few coal miners become supervisors, but additional training is required for supervisory and management jobs.

After a period of on-the-job experience, coal mining technicians may become supervisors, sales representatives, or possibly even private consultants or special service contractors.

Technical sales representatives work for manufacturers of mining equipment and supplies and sell such products as explosives, flotation chemicals, rock drills, hoists, crushers, grinding mills, classifiers, materials handling equipment, and safety equipment.

## EARNINGS

According to 2009 data from the DOL, continuous mining-machine operators earned a median salary of $46,920 per year, with the lowest paid 10 percent making less than $31,470 and the highest paid 10 percent making more than $62,110 annually. Mine cutting and channeling machine operators earned salaries that ranged from less than $28,750 to $56,720 or more. These workers earned a median annual salary of $43,010. Those with considerable experience have even higher earnings.

Among coal miners, earnings vary according to experience and type of mine. Highest paid are seasoned workers in deep underground mines. Coal miners at strip and auger mines are paid slightly less. Utility workers and unskilled laborers at coal preparation plants earn the lowest salaries. Additionally, unionized workers typically earn higher salaries than coal miners who are not members of a union.

These figures do not include overtime or incentive pay. Miners get time and a half or double time for overtime hours. Coal miners who work evening and night shifts typically receive slightly higher wages.

Most coal miners also receive health and life insurance, as well as pension benefits. The insurance generally includes hospitalization, surgery, convalescent care, rehabilitation services, and maternity benefits for the workers and their dependents. The pension size depends on the worker's age at retirement and the number of years of service.

In addition, most mine workers are given 11 holidays a year in addition to vacation days earned according to length of service.

## WORK ENVIRONMENT

Coal mining is hard work involving harsh and sometimes hazardous conditions. Workers in surface mines are outdoors in all kinds of weather, while those underground work in tunnels that are cramped, dark, dusty, wet, and cold. They are all subjected to loud noise from the machinery and work that is physically demanding and dirty.

Since passage of the Coal Mine Health and Safety Act in 1969, mine operators have improved the ventilation and lighting in underground mines and have taken steps to eliminate safety hazards for workers. Nevertheless, operators of the heavy machinery both on the surface and below ground run the risk of injury or death from accidents. Other possible hazards for underground miners include roof falls and cave-ins, poisonous and explosive gases, and long exposure to coal dust. After a number of years, workers may develop pneumoconiosis, or "black lung," which is a disabling and sometimes fatal disease.

## OUTLOOK

Employment in mining is expected to decline by about 14 percent through 2018, according to the DOL. Technological advances have increased productivity but reduced the number of workers in the field. Stricter federal environmental regulations, such as the 1990 Clean Air Act Amendments, and increased competition from foreign producers will limit growth in this industry. Despite this prediction, there should continue to be opportunities for coal miners, since coal remains the primary fuel source for electricity generation.

Because coal is a major resource for the production of such products as steel and cement, employment in the mining industry is strongly affected by changes in the overall economy. In a recession the demand for coal drops and many miners may be laid off.

## FOR MORE INFORMATION

*For free student materials (booklets, brochures, posters, videos, online publications) about coal, electricity, and land reclamation issues, contact*
American Coal Foundation
101 Constitution Avenue, NW, Suite 525 East
Washington, DC 20001-2133

Tel: 202-463-9785
E-mail: info@teachcoal.org
http://www.teachcoal.org

*For information on mine safety and legislation enacted to protect workers in the industry, contact*
Mine Safety and Health Administration
1100 Wilson Boulevard, 21st Floor
Arlington, VA 22209-3939
Tel: 202-693-9400
http://www.msha.gov

*For statistics on the mining industry, contact*
National Mining Association
101 Constitution Avenue, NW, Suite 500 East
Washington, DC 20001-2133
Tel: 202-463-2600
http://www.nma.org

*For information on educational programs, contact*
Society for Mining, Metallurgy, and Exploration
8307 Shaffer Parkway
Littleton, CO 80127-4102
Tel: 800-763-3132
http://www.smenet.org

*The following labor union represents coal miners. For information on publications, press releases, and other resources, contact*
United Mine Workers of America
18354 Quantico Gateway Drive, Suite 200
Triangle, VA 22172-1179
Tel: 703-291-2400
http://www.umwa.org

# Energy Conservation Technicians

## OVERVIEW

*Energy conservation technicians*, also known as *energy auditors*, identify and measure the amount of energy used to heat, cool, and operate a building or industrial process. They analyze the efficiency of energy use and determine the amount of energy lost through wasteful processes or lack of insulation. After analysis, they suggest energy conservation techniques and install any needed corrective measures.

## HISTORY

At the start of the 20th century, energy costs were only a fraction of the total expense of operating homes, offices, and factories. Coal and petroleum were abundant and relatively inexpensive. Low energy prices contributed to the emergence of the United States as the leading industrialized nation as well as the world's largest energy consumer.

Because petroleum was inexpensive and could easily produce heat, steam, electricity, and fuel, it displaced coal for many purposes. As a result, the nation's coal mining industry declined, and the United States became dependent on foreign oil for half of its energy supply.

In 1973, when many foreign oil-producing nations stopped shipments of oil to the United States and other Western countries, fuel costs increased dramatically. More recently, political instability in the Middle East—where many of the top oil-producing countries are located—caused fuel prices to rise significantly once again. This uncertainty regarding supply and a growing awareness about environmental pollution

A technician conducts an energy audit at a customer's home. He is checking for air leakage. *(Dick Blume, Syracuse Newspapers/The Image Works)*

have fueled the development of energy conservation techniques in the United States. The emphasis on discovering new sources of energy, developing more efficient methods and equipment to use energy, and reducing the amount of wasted energy has created a demand for energy conservation technicians.

## THE JOB

Energy efficiency and conservation are major concerns in nearly all homes and workplaces. This means that work assignments for energy conservation technicians vary greatly. They may inspect homes, businesses, or industrial buildings to identify conditions that cause energy waste, recommend ways to reduce the waste, and help install corrective measures. When technicians complete an analysis of a problem in energy use and effectiveness, they can state the results in tangible dollar costs, losses, or savings. Their work provides a basis for important decisions on using and conserving energy.

Energy conservation technicians may be employed in power plants, research laboratories, construction firms, industrial facilities, government agencies, or companies that sell and service equipment.

The jobs these technicians perform can be divided into four major areas of energy activity: research and development, production, use, and conservation.

In research and development, technicians usually work in laboratories testing mechanical, electrical, chemical, pneumatic, hydraulic, thermal, or optical scientific principles. Typical employers include institutions, private industry, government, and the military. Working under the direction of an engineer, physicist, chemist, or metallurgist, technicians use specialized equipment and materials to perform laboratory experiments. They help record data and analyze it using computers. They may also be responsible for periodic maintenance and repair of equipment.

In energy production, typical employers include solar energy equipment manufacturers, installers, and users; power plants; and process plants that use high-temperature heat, steam, or water. Technicians in this field work with engineers and managers to develop, install, operate, maintain, and repair systems and devices used for the conversion of fuels or other resources into useful energy. Such plants may produce hot water, steam, mechanical motion, or electrical power through systems such as furnaces, electrical power plants, and solar heating systems. These systems may be controlled manually by semiautomated control panels or by computers.

## Tips on Saving Energy

Try the following to save energy and money:

- Ask your parents to perform an energy survey or audit of your home to find ways to reduce utility bills each month.
- At home, dress warmer in the winter and cooler in the summer to help reduce heating and cooling costs.
- Turn off lights and appliances when you are finished using them.
- Ask your parents to replace regular light bulbs with compact fluorescent lights, which use about one-fourth of the energy of regular light bulbs.
- Ride your bike or walk to school and other activities to save gas and reduce pollution.
- Recycle plastics, glass, steel and aluminum cans, and newspapers.
- Purchase products that are made of recycled material.

Source: U.S. Department of Energy

In the field of energy use, technicians might work to improve efficiency in industrial engineering and production line equipment. They also maintain equipment and buildings for hospitals, schools, and multifamily housing.

Technicians employed in energy conservation typically work for manufacturing companies, consulting engineers, energy-audit firms, and energy-audit departments of public utility companies. Municipal governments, hotels, architects, private builders, and manufacturers of heating, ventilating, and air-conditioning equipment also hire them. Working in teams under engineers, technicians determine building specifications, modify equipment and structures, audit energy use and the efficiency of machines and systems, then recommend modifications or changes to save energy.

If working for a utility company, a technician might work as part of a demand-side management (DSM) program, which helps customers reduce the amount of their electric bill. Under DSM programs, energy conservation technicians visit customers' homes to interview them about household energy use, such as the type of heating system, the number of people home during the day, the furnace temperature setting, and prior heating costs.

Technicians then draw a sketch of the house, measure its perimeter, windows, and doors, and record dimensions on the sketch. They inspect attics, crawl spaces, and basements and note any loose-fitting windows, uninsulated pipes, and deficient insulation. They read hot-water tank labels to find the heat-loss rating and determine the need for a tank insulation blanket. Technicians also examine air furnace filters and heat exchangers to detect dirt or soot buildup that might affect furnace operations. Once technicians identify a problem, they must know how to correct it. After discussing problems with the customer, the technician recommends repairs and provides literature on conservation improvements and sources of loans.

## REQUIREMENTS

### High School

If you are interested in this field, take classes such as algebra, geometry, physics, chemistry, machine shop, and ecology. These courses and others incorporating laboratory work will provide you with a solid foundation for any postsecondary program that follows. In addition, classes in computer science, drafting (either mechanical or architectural), and public speaking are also very helpful.

## Postsecondary Training

Many community colleges and technical institutes offer two-year programs under the specific title of energy conservation and use technology or energy management technology. In addition, schools offer related programs in solar power, electric power, building maintenance, equipment maintenance, and general engineering technology. Though not required for many entry-level jobs, these postsecondary programs can expand career options. With an advanced degree, applicants have a better chance at higher paying jobs, often with private industries.

Advanced training focuses on the principles and applications of physics, energy conservation, energy economics, instrumentation, electronics, electromechanical systems, computers, heating systems, and air-conditioning. A typical curriculum offers a first year of study in physics, chemistry, mathematics, energy technology, energy production systems, electricity and electromechanical devices, and microcomputer operations. The second year of study becomes more specialized, including courses in mechanical and fluid systems, electrical power, blueprint reading, energy conservation, codes and regulations, technical communications, and energy audits.

Considerable time is spent in laboratories, where students gain hands-on experience by assembling, disassembling, adjusting, and operating devices, mechanisms, and integrated systems of machines and controls.

## Certification or Licensing

There are no state or federal requirements for certification or licensing of energy conservation technicians. However, certification from the National Institute for Certification in Engineering Technologies and a degree from an accredited technical program are valuable credentials and proof of knowledge and technical skills. The Association of Energy Engineers offers various certifications to professionals in the field, and North American Technician Excellence (http://www.natex.org) offers an energy efficiency certification specialization for heating and cooling industry technicians.

## Other Requirements

Students entering this field must have a practical understanding of the physical sciences, a good aptitude for math, and the ability to communicate in writing and speech with technical specialists as well as the average consumer. Their work requires a clear and precise understanding of operational and maintenance manuals, schematic drawings, blueprints, and computational formulas.

Some positions in electrical power plants require energy conservation technicians to pass certain psychological tests to predict their behavior during crises. Security clearances, arranged by the employer, are required for employment in nuclear power plants and other workplaces designated by the government as high-security facilities.

## EXPLORING

To learn more about this profession, ask your career counselor for additional information or for assistance in arranging a field trip to an industrial, commercial, or business workplace to explore energy efficiency.

Utility companies exist in almost every city and employ energy analysts or a team of auditors in their customer service departments. Energy specialists also work for large hospitals, office buildings, hotels, universities, and manufacturing plants. Contact these employers of energy technicians to learn about opportunities for volunteer, part-time, or summer work.

You can also enroll in seminars offered by community colleges or equipment and material suppliers to learn about such topics as building insulation and energy sources. Student projects in energy conservation or part-time work with social service agencies that help low-income citizens meet their energy costs are other options for exploration.

## EMPLOYERS

Energy conservation technicians are employed in areas where much energy is used, such as power plants, research laboratories, construction firms, industrial facilities, government agencies, and companies that sell and service equipment. Technicians who focus on research and development work for institutions, private industry, government, and the military. Those who work in energy use are employed by manufacturing facilities, consulting engineering firms, energy audit firms, and energy audit departments of utility companies. Other employers include municipal governments, manufacturers of heating and cooling equipment, private builders, hotels, and architects.

## STARTING OUT

Most graduates of technical programs are able to secure jobs in energy conservation before graduation by working with their schools' career services offices. Placement staffs work closely with potential employers, especially those that have hired graduates in recent years. Many large companies schedule regular recruiting visits to schools before graduation.

It is also possible to enter the field of energy conservation on the basis of work experience. People with a background in construction, plumbing, insulation, or heating may enter this field with the help of additional training to supplement their past work experience. Training in military instrumentation and systems control and maintenance is also good preparation for the prospective energy conservation technician. Former navy technicians are particularly sought in the field of energy production.

Opportunities for on-the-job training in energy conservation are available through part-time or summer work in hospitals, major office buildings, hotel chains, and universities. Some regions have youth corps aimed at high school students, such as the Corporation for Youth Energy Corps (CYEC) in New York City's South Bronx. The CYEC offers those who did not complete high school the option of combining work experience and school to earn a general equivalency diploma, get a job, or both.

Some jobs in energy production, such as those in electrical power plants, can be obtained right out of high school. New employees, however, are expected to successfully complete company-sponsored training courses to keep up to date and advance to positions with more responsibility. Graduates with associate's degrees in energy conservation and use, instrumentation, electronics, or electro-mechanical technology will normally enter employment at a higher level, with more responsibility and higher pay, than those with less education. Jobs in energy research and development almost always require an associate's degree.

## ADVANCEMENT

Because the career is relatively new, well-established patterns of advancement have not yet emerged. Nevertheless, technicians in any of the four areas of energy conservation can advance to higher positions, such as senior and supervisory positions. These advanced positions require a combination of formal education, work experience, and special seminars or classes usually sponsored or paid for by the employer.

Technicians can also advance by progressing to new, more challenging assignments. For example, hotels, restaurants, and retail stores hire experienced energy technicians to manage energy consumption. This often involves visits to each location to audit and examine its facilities or procedures to see where energy use can be reduced. The technician then provides training in energy-saving practices. Other experienced energy technicians may be employed as sales and customer service representatives for producers of power, energy, special control systems, or equipment designed to improve energy efficiency.

Technicians with experience and money to invest may start their own businesses, selling energy-saving products, providing audits, or recommending energy-efficient renovations.

## EARNINGS

Earnings of energy conservation technicians vary significantly based on their amount of formal training and experience. According to the U.S. Department of Labor (DOL), the average annual salary for environmental engineering technicians in engineering and architectural services was $43,520 in 2009. Salaries for all environmental engineering technicians ranged from less than $27,160 to $70,840 or more annually.

Technicians typically receive paid vacations, group insurance benefits, and employee retirement plans. In addition, their employers often offer financial support for all or part of continuing educational programs, which are necessary in order for technicians to keep up to date with technological changes that occur in this developing field.

## WORK ENVIRONMENT

Because energy conservation technicians are employed in many different settings, the environment in which they work varies widely. Energy conservation technicians employed in research and development, design, or product planning generally work in laboratories or engineering departments with normal daytime work schedules. Other technicians often travel to customer locations or work in their employer's plant.

Work in energy production and use requires around-the-clock shifts. In these two areas, technicians work either indoors or outdoors at the employer's site. Such assignments require little or no travel, but the work environments may be dirty, noisy, or affected by the weather. Appropriate work clothing must be worn in shop and factory settings, and safety awareness and safe working habits must be practiced at all times.

Energy conservation technicians who work in a plant usually interact with only a small group of people, but those who work for utility companies may have to communicate with the public while providing technical services to their customers. Energy research and development jobs involve laboratory activities requiring social inter-action with engineers, scientists, and other technicians. In some cases, technicians may be considered public relations representatives, which may call for special attention to dress and overall appearance.

Job stress varies depending on the job. The pace is relaxed but businesslike in engineering, planning, and design departments and in research and development. However, in more hectic areas, techni-cians must respond to crisis situations involving unexpected break-downs of equipment that must be corrected as soon as possible.

## OUTLOOK

Since energy use constitutes a major expense for industry, commerce, government, institutions, and private citizens, the demand for energy conservation technicians is likely to remain strong. The DOL pre-dicts that the employment of environmental engineering technicians is expected to increase much faster than the average for all occupa-tions through 2018. In addition to the financial costs of purchasing natural resources, the added reality of the physical costs of depleting these important resources continues to create a greater demand for trained energy conservation employees. However, employment is influenced by local and national economic conditions.

The utilities industry is in the midst of significant regulatory and institutional changes. Government regulations are moving utility companies toward deregulation, opening new avenues for energy service companies. In the past, energy conservation programs have been dominated by people with engineering and other technical skills. These skills will remain important, but as the industry becomes more customer focused, there will be a growing need for more people with marketing and financial skills.

Utility companies, manufacturers, and government agencies are working together to establish energy efficiency standards. The Con-sortium for Energy Efficiency (http://www.cee1.org) is a collabora-tive effort involving a group of electric and gas utility companies, government energy agencies, and environmental groups working to develop programs aimed at improving energy efficiency in commercial air-conditioning equipment, lighting, geothermal heat pumps, and other systems. Programs such as these will create job opportunities for technicians.

Utility DSM programs, which have traditionally concentrated on the residential sector, are now focusing more attention on industrial and commercial facilities. With the goal of realizing larger energy savings, lower costs, and more permanent energy-efficient changes, DSM programs are expanding to work with contractors, builders, retailers, distributors, and manufacturers, creating more demand for technicians.

## FOR MORE INFORMATION

*For information on environmental careers and degree programs, contact*
Advanced Technology Environmental and Energy Center
500 Belmont Road
Bettendorf, IA 52722-5649
http://www.ateec.org

*For information on energy conservation, contact*
Association of Energy Conservation Professionals
The Jacksonville Center
220 Parkway Lane, Box 5A
Floyd, VA 24091-4171
Tel: 540-745-2838
E-mail: aecp@swva.net
http://www.aecpes.org

*For information on technical seminars, certification programs, conferences, books, and journals, contact*
Association of Energy Engineers
4025 Pleasantdale Road, Suite 420
Atlanta, GA 30340-4260
Tel: 770-447-5083
http://www.aeecenter.org

*For information on energy efficiency and renewable energy, visit the following Web site:*
Energy Efficiency and Renewable Energy
U.S. Department of Energy
Mail Stop EE-1
Washington, DC 20585
http://www1.eere.energy.gov/education

*For information on certification programs for engineering technicians and technologists, contact*
National Institute for Certification in Engineering Technologies
1420 King Street
Alexandria, VA 22314-2794
Tel: 888-476-4238
http://www.nicet.org

# Energy Transmission and Distribution Workers

## OVERVIEW

*Energy transmission and distribution workers* are employed in the electric light and power industry. They operate and maintain power-regulating equipment and networks of high-voltage power lines that send electricity from power plants to domestic, industrial, and commercial users.

## HISTORY

Electricity was developed as a source of power during the 19th century when a variety of technological advances made large-scale production of electricity feasible. The development of the first electric light bulb played an important role in the early growth of the electric power industry. Thomas Edison demonstrated his first carbon filament lamp in 1879, and by 1882 the first permanent, commercial electric power-generating plant and distribution network was established in New York City. Other generating plants and power line networks soon followed throughout Europe and America. These early systems proved to be inefficient at transmitting power over long distances because they used direct electric current, but generators that produced alternating current became practical in the 1890s. Many new uses for electric power were developed, and

### QUICK FACTS

**School Subjects**
Physics
Technical/shop

**Personal Skills**
Following instructions
Mechanical/manipulative

**Work Environment**
Indoors and outdoors
One location with some travel

**Minimum Education Level**
High school diploma

**Salary Range**
$32,170 to $66,990 to $100,310+

**Certification or Licensing**
Required for certain positions (certification)
Required for certain positions (licensing)

**Outlook**
Little or no change (power plant operators, distributors, and dispatchers)
More slowly than the average (line installers)

**DOT**
821, 829, 952

**GOE**
08.06.01

*(continues)*

by the early 1900s, electric-powered devices were increasingly common in homes, businesses, and factories across the United States.

Other advances, such as the development of oil-insulated transformers, also contributed to delivering electric power over great distances. In 1914, it was possible to send 150,000 volts over aerial transmission lines. There were problems, however, in the underground transmission of power. Several procedures were tried and dismissed, but the development of lead-sheathed cable in 1925 made it possible to transmit more than 100,000 volts underground.

Today, electric power generated at central power stations is sent to substations, then on to consumers via overhead lines, underground and submarine cables, and microwave systems. At generating stations or nearby substations, voltages must be stepped up so that less power is lost through resistance as the electricity is transmitted over long distances. Transformers in substations at the end of long transmission lines must decrease voltage to levels that are suitable for distribution to users.

## THE JOB

Various workers are involved in regulating and directing electric power as it flows from the generators to consumers. The basic concern these workers share is maintaining a continuous and uninterrupted flow of energy, regardless of changing conditions and any problems that arise in the transmission and distribution system.

*Substation operators* monitor and regulate the flow of electricity at various facilities. At some substations located close to power plants, voltage may be stepped up for long distance transmission. Operators at these substations observe and record readings of instruments and meters that provide data on the electricity as it comes into and flows out of the substation.

At other substations at the end of long lines, where the voltage is stepped down again, the operators ensure that the equipment reduces the voltage for use by local consumers. Substation operators keep in touch with the main generating plant and connect or break the flow of electricity using levers that control circuit breakers. In substations where alternating current is changed to direct current to meet needs of special users, operators control converters that make these changes.

Some operators monitor equipment at several substations. Increasingly, the activities of substation operators are being automated so that the flow of electricity at various substations can be monitored and regulated from a central location.

*Power distributors and dispatchers,* also called *load dispatchers* or *systems operators,* control the transmission of power that is sent out from power plants. They work in rooms that function like command posts for coordinating the generating and distributing activities. These dispatchers monitor readings at a map, or pilot board, which is like an automated map that displays everything that is happening throughout the entire transmission system. Instruments, meters, and lights on the pilot board show the status of transmission circuits, connections with substations, and the power draw by large industrial users. Based on this information, load dispatchers operate current converters, voltage transformers, and circuit breakers.

They also anticipate power needs, based on previous patterns of power use and variable factors such as weather conditions, and inform operators in the central control room of the generating plant about how much power will be needed at a later time. For example, if a hot day is forecast, load dispatchers know that consumers will be putting air-conditioners, fans, and refrigerators to maximum use and that enough power will have to be generated to meet the demand. In other instances, they may tell control room operators to produce less electricity when demand levels drop. In the event of emergencies such as equipment failures, they redirect the power flow around the problem until the situation is corrected. They may also operate equipment to adjust voltage up or down at substations and to control power flow in and out of the substations.

*Line installers,* also known as *utility lineworkers,* install, maintain, and repair poles, power lines, and other equipment that is part of the system for transmitting and distributing electricity from power plants to substations and to consumers. They may work alone or with small crews. To install poles in the ground, they may use power equipment to dig holes and set in the poles. Line installers ride buckets on trucks with pneumatic lifts or sometimes climb the telephone poles to attach wires and cables to poles. Other responsibilities may include bolting or clamping insulators, lightning arresters, transformers, circuit breakers, switches, or other equipment.

With the help of other workers, installers string wires between poles or to buildings, adjusting the slack so that the lines do not break in changing weather conditions. They splice cables and attach wires to auxiliary equipment, using various hand tools. For underground cable installations, they may need to dig holes using special power equipment, such as trenchers and plows. Electric companies often contract out the job of installing high transmission towers to companies that specialize in such jobs, but utility lineworkers also may be involved in this work.

*Ground helpers* aid in setting up electric lines. Working as members of installation and repair crews, they dig holes, raise poles, and string lines. They may also pass the correct tools and equipment to installers and compact earth around the base of newly erected poles to hold them firmly in place.

*Troubleshooters* are experienced lineworkers who respond to emergency situations that require quick diagnosis and repair. They must be familiar with the power system and the various kinds of malfunctions that may develop. When they receive a call from a dispatcher, troubleshooters go to the area where the malfunction is reported. They examine the equipment and use testing devices to locate and assess the problem. They repair or replace conductors, switches, fuses, transformers, and related equipment. When they work with electrically energized lines, they use special safety methods and insulated ladders, tools, and platforms.

*Cable splicers* install and repair cables, especially in urban areas where cables are installed underground because above-ground power lines are impractical. Cable splicers pull cable through conduits, or ducts, that contain wires and join the cables at connecting points, according to diagrams and specifications. Also, they insulate the splice and seal it with a protective covering. They use testing devices to detect broken cables and incorrect connections, and they reinsulate or replace defective connections and cables.

## REQUIREMENTS

### High School

For entry-level positions such as lineworkers, employers generally prefer high school graduates who can demonstrate mechanical aptitude and good mathematical, verbal, and reasoning skills on tests they administer. Applicants may also need to pass physical tests of balance, coordination, and strength. In high school, take courses in electrical shop, machine shop, drafting, and applied sciences.

### Postsecondary Training

Utility lineworkers and cable splicers usually learn their skills in apprenticeship programs, which are administered jointly by employers and unions that organize company workers. Apprenticeships, which last up to five years, combine on-the-job training with formal instruction in related subjects. Apprentices attend classes to learn such subjects as blueprint reading, electrical theory, transmission theory, electrical codes, and job safety practices. In many programs, apprentices supplement class work with educational videos and computer-assisted instructional materials. They also get practical experience as helpers to experienced lineworkers. They begin by doing simple tasks and, as they learn, take on progressively more difficult work.

Load dispatchers and substation operators need a background that includes good training in sciences and mathematics, as well as years of job experience with the company. Although dispatchers and operators with only a high school diploma will be able to find positions, the best jobs will go to those with college-level training.

Some energy transmission and distribution workers earn certificates or associate's degrees in electronics or related fields from community colleges.

## Certification or Licensing

Power distributors and dispatchers whose work may affect the power grid must be certified by the North American Energy Reliability Corporation. The organization offers the following certification designations: reliability operator, balancing and interchange operator, transmission operator, and balancing, interchange, and transmission operator.

Some power plant operators, distributors, and dispatchers must be licensed. Requirements vary by state and type of employer. Check with your state's department of licensing and professional regulation for information on requirements in your state.

## Other Requirements

You should be comfortable working at heights and in confined spaces. You also need to have good color vision to be able to distinguish color-coded wires and have a basic understanding of the principles of electricity. Since many positions in this field involve extensive bending, climbing, reaching, and other physical exertion, workers should be in good physical condition in order to withstand the rigors of the job. Other important traits include attention to detail, organizational skills, the ability to solve problems, and the ability to work as a member of a team and on one's own as necessary.

## EXPLORING

You can pursue your interest in subjects related to these occupations by taking courses such as physics and drafting. Shop courses can provide you with an opportunity to work with electrical and mechanical devices and to develop skills in schematic drawing. Some power plants have visitors' centers where the public is allowed to observe some of the plant operations and to learn how electricity is generated and distributed to consumers.

## EMPLOYERS

Approximately 50,400 power plant operators, distributors, and dispatchers are employed in the United States. Electrical power-line installers and repairers hold about 133,900 jobs. Electric light and power companies typically employ energy transmission and distribution workers. They may find jobs anywhere there is a power plant. Manufacturing plants that produce electricity for their own use employ other workers.

## STARTING OUT

Load dispatchers and substation operators usually start off in other positions, perhaps entering as helpers or assistants. Depending on the openings that develop, the workers' preferences, and results of aptitude tests, they may be assigned to training for work as a substation operator. Load dispatchers may be chosen from among experienced substation operators. The training for load dispatchers is extensive, lasting several years. After completing initial training, dispatchers usually participate in periodic refresher training to update their skills.

## ADVANCEMENT

Advancement in these occupations is often related to amount of experience and to receiving additional training at the company. Thus, with experience and training, ground helpers, for example, can become utility lineworkers. Experienced lineworkers, including utility lineworkers and cable splicers, may be promoted to supervisory positions. Expert utility lineworkers may become troubleshooters.

Load dispatchers and substation operators are promoted to these positions from other jobs inside the plant. Most of these workers continue to advance within the same plant or utility and eventually may become shift supervisors.

# EARNINGS

Earnings of energy transmission and distribution workers vary considerably depending on specific job responsibilities, length of service with the company, geographic region, and other factors.

The U.S. Department of Labor (DOL) reports that median annual earnings of power plant operators were $60,400 in 2009. Salaries ranged from less than $39,520 to more than $82,770 a year. Nuclear power reactor operators' salaries ranged from less than $54,590 for the lowest paid 10 percent to more than $100,310 for the highest paid 10 percent, with a median of $72,650. Power distributors and dispatchers earned salaries that ranged from less than $46,130 to $89,510 or more, with a median of $66,990 in 2009.

Electrical power line installers earned salaries that ranged from less than $32,170 to $80,310 or more in 2009, according to the DOL. Utility line workers and other workers who are union members generally have their pay rates set according to agreements between the union and their employer. The agreements cover many factors, such as wage increases and pay rates for different categories of overtime work. Overtime pay can add significantly to base salary. In addition to their regular earnings, these workers receive benefits such as paid vacation time, pension plans, and life and health insurance.

# WORK ENVIRONMENT

Workers who install and repair electric power lines encounter a variety of conditions on the job. They often work outdoors in all kinds of weather. They may have to climb to high places or work in awkward positions, such as stooped over in damp underground tunnels. They may have to lift heavy cables. As they work, they must always be aware of safety issues and follow procedures that minimize the risk of injury. Lines energized with electricity can cause burns or fatal electric shocks. Workers who go into underground tunnels have to use special safety equipment and test for the presence of explosive or poisonous gas in the air. Some workers risk being exposed to hazardous chemicals in solvents and other materials. Other potential risks include being hit by objects falling from overhead at a work site.

Even during their off hours, installation and repair workers may have to be available for emergency repairs. After a major storm, for example, they may have to work long hours and travel great distances to help repair equipment and restore service to customers.

In facilities where power flow is monitored and regulated, workers enjoy clean, orderly, well-lighted, and ventilated control rooms. Their work is not strenuous, but they must constantly pay attention to the equipment that indicates how the system is functioning. Since electricity must be provided to consumers all the time, they must work some shifts at night, on weekends, and on holidays, often on a rotating basis.

## OUTLOOK

Little or no employment change is expected for power plant operators, distributors, and dispatchers through 2018, according to the DOL. Despite this prediction, there will be excellent opportunities in the field as a result of a growing demand for electricity in the United States and the construction of new power plants. A large number of retiring workers will also create many openings for new workers. Faster-than-average growth is predicted for nuclear power plant operators.

Employment for electrical line installers and repairers is expected to grow more slowly than the average. Despite this prediction, there will be many job openings. Much work that power utility lineworkers do is not as readily automated, and many openings for these workers will continue to develop as experienced workers transfer to other jobs or leave the workforce.

Job growth may be tempered in part because of industry deregulation and increased competition between electric light and power companies. In addition, technological improvements have made some equipment more efficient and reliable, and the use of automatic controls is reducing the need for people to monitor and regulate transmission and distribution systems.

## FOR MORE INFORMATION

*For statistics and other information about the public power industry, contact*
American Public Power Association
1875 Connecticut Avenue, NW, Suite 1200
Washington, DC 20009-5715
Tel: 800-515-2772
http://www.publicpower.org

*For information on careers, contact*
Center for Energy Workforce Development
701 Pennsylvania Avenue, NW
Washington, DC 20004-2696

Tel: 202-638-5802
E-mail: staff@cewd.org
http://www.cewd.org

*For information on energy issues and a list of available publications, contact*
**Edison Electric Institute**
701 Pennsylvania Avenue, NW
Washington, DC 20004-2696
Tel: 202-508-5000
http://www.eei.org

*For information on union representation, contact*
**International Brotherhood of Electrical Workers**
900 Seventh Street, NW
Washington, DC 20001-3886
Tel: 202-833-7000
http://www.ibew.org

*For information on certification, contact*
**North American Electric Reliability Corporation**
116-390 Village Boulevard
Princeton, NJ 08540-5721
Tel: 609-452-8060
http://www.nerc.com

*For information on careers and training, visit*
**Get Into Energy**
http://www.getintoenergy.com

*For a full overview of the energy industry, visit*
**U.S. Energy Information Administration: Energy Kids**
http://www.eia.doe.gov/kids

# Geologists

## QUICK FACTS

**School Subjects**
Earth science
Geography

**Personal Skills**
Helping/teaching
Technical/scientific

**Work Environment**
Indoors and outdoors
One location with some
travel

**Minimum Education Level**
Bachelor's degree

**Salary Range**
$43,140 to $81,220 to
$161,260+

**Certification or Licensing**
Voluntary (certification)
Required by certain states
(licensing)

**Outlook**
Faster than the average

**DOT**
024

**GOE**
02.02.01

**NOC**
2113

**O*NET-SOC**
19-2042.01

## OVERVIEW

*Geologists* study all aspects of the earth, including its origin, history, composition, and structure. Along more practical lines, geologists may, through the use of theoretical knowledge and research data, locate groundwater, oil, minerals, and other natural resources. They play an increasingly important role in studying, preserving, and cleaning up the environment. They advise construction companies and government agencies on the suitability of locations being considered for buildings, highways, and other structures. They also prepare geological reports, maps, and diagrams. There are approximately 33,600 geoscientists (which includes geologists, geophysicists, and oceanographers) employed in the United States.

## HISTORY

Geology is a young science, first developed by early mining engineers. In the late 18th century, scientists such as A. G. Werner and James Hutton, a retired British physician, created a sensation with their differing theories on the origins of rocks. Through the study of fossils and the development of geological maps, others continued to examine the history of the earth in the 19th century.

From these beginnings, geology has made rapid advances, both in scope and knowledge. With the development of more intricate technology, geologists are able to study areas of the earth they were previously unable to reach. Seismographs, for example, measure energy waves resulting from the earth's movement in order to determine the location and intensity of earthquakes. Seismic prospecting involves bouncing sound waves off buried rock layers.

# THE JOB

The geologist's work includes locating and obtaining physical data and material. This may necessitate the drilling of deep holes to

A geologist studies maps while working on a geological mapping project. (Jim Cole, AP Photo)

obtain samples, the collection and examination of the materials found on or under the earth's surface, or the use of instruments to measure the earth's gravity and magnetic field. Some geologists may spend three to six months of each year conducting fieldwork. In laboratory work, geologists carry out studies based on field research. Sometimes working under controlled temperatures or pressures, geologists analyze the chemical and physical properties of geological specimens, such as rock, fossil remains, and soil. Once the data is analyzed and the studies are completed, geologists and geological technicians write reports based on their research.

A wide variety of laboratory instruments are used, including X-ray diffractometers, which determine the crystal structure of minerals, and petrographic microscopes for the study of rock and sediment samples.

Geologists working to protect the environment may design and monitor waste disposal sites, preserve water supplies, and reclaim contaminated land and water to comply with federal environmental regulations.

Geologists often specialize in one of the following two main branches of the field: physical geology and historical geology.

## Physical Geology

*Economic geologists* search for new resources of minerals and fuels.

*Engineering geologists* are responsible for the application of geological knowledge to problems arising in the construction of roads, buildings, bridges, dams, and other structures.

*Environmental geologists* study how pollution, waste, hazardous materials, and flooding and erosion affect the earth.

*Geohydrologists,* also known as *hydrogeologists,* study the nature and distribution of water within the earth and are often involved in environmental impact studies.

*Geomorphologists* study the form of the earth's surface and the processes, such as erosion and glaciation, that bring about changes.

*Geophysicists* are concerned with matter and energy and how they interact. They study the physical properties and structure of the earth, from its interior to its upper atmosphere, including land surfaces, subsurfaces, and bodies of water.

*Glacial geologists* study the physical properties and movement of ice sheets and glaciers.

*Marine geologists* study the oceans, including the seabed and subsurface features. They are also known as *geological oceanographers.*

*Mineralogists* are interested in the classification of minerals composing rocks and mineral deposits. To this end, they examine and analyze the physical and chemical properties of minerals and precious stones to develop data and theories on their origin, occurrence, and possible uses in industry and commerce.

*Petroleum geologists* are economic geologists who attempt to locate natural gas and oil deposits through exploratory testing and study of the data obtained. They recommend the acquisition of new properties and the retention or release of properties already owned by their companies. They also estimate oil reserves and assist petroleum engineers in determining exact production procedures.

*Petrologists* study the origin and composition of igneous, metamorphic, and sedimentary rocks. (See the article Petrologists for more information.)

*Seismologists* study earthquake shocks and their effects.

*Structural geologists* investigate the stresses and strains in the earth's crust and the deformations they produce.

The geologist is far from limited in a choice of work, but a basic knowledge of all sciences is essential in each of these specializations. An increasing number of scientists combine geology with detailed knowledge in another field. *Geochemists,* for example, are concerned with the chemical composition of, and the changes in, minerals and rocks, while *planetary geologists* apply their knowledge of geology to interpret surface conditions on other planets and the moon.

## Historical Geology

*Geochronologists* are geoscientists who use radioactive dating and other techniques to estimate the age of rock and other samples from an exploration site.

*Paleontologists* specialize in the study of the earth's rock formations, including remains of plant and animal life, in order to understand the earth's evolution and estimate its age.

*Sedimentologists,* also known as sedimentary geologists, study sediments such silt, sand, and mud. These sediments often contain coal, gas, oil, and mineral deposits. Closely related to sedimentologists are *stratigraphers.* Stratigraphers study the distribution and relative arrangement of sedimentary rock layers. This enables them to understand evolutionary changes in fossils and plants, which leads to an understanding of successive changes in the distribution of land and sea.

# REQUIREMENTS
## High School
Because you will need a college degree in order to find work in this profession, you should take a college preparatory curriculum while

in high school. Such a curriculum will include computer science, history, English, and geography classes. Science and math classes are also important to take, particularly earth science, chemistry, and physics. Math classes should include algebra, trigonometry, and statistics.

## Postsecondary Training

A bachelor's degree is the minimum requirement for entry into lower-level geology jobs, but a master's degree is usually necessary for beginning positions in research, teaching, and exploration. A person with a strong background in physics, chemistry, mathematics, or computer science may also qualify for some geology jobs. For those wishing to make significant advancements in research and in teaching at the college level, a doctoral degree is required. Those interested in the geological profession should have an aptitude not only for geology but also for physics, chemistry, and mathematics.

A number of colleges, universities, and institutions of technology offer degrees in geology. Programs in geophysical technology, geophysical engineering, geophysical prospecting, and engineering geology also offer related training for beginning geologists.

Traditional geoscience courses emphasize classical geologic methods and concepts. Mineralogy, paleontology, stratigraphy, and structural geology are important courses for undergraduates. Students interested in environmental and regulatory fields should take courses in hydrology, hazardous waste management, environmental legislation, chemistry, fluid mechanics, and geologic logging.

In addition, students should take courses in related sciences, mathematics, English composition, and computer science. Students seeking graduate degrees in geology should concentrate on advanced courses in geology, placing major emphasis on their particular fields.

## Certification or Licensing

The American Institute of Professional Geologists (AIPG) grants the certified professional geologist (CPG) designation to geologists who have earned a bachelor's degree or higher in the geological sciences and have eight years of professional experience (applicants with a master's degree need only seven years of professional experience and those with a Ph.D., five years). Candidates must also undergo peer review by three professional geologists (two of whom must be CPGs) and pay an application fee.

The institute also offers the member designation to geologists who are registered in various states and are not seeking AIPG certification. Applicants must have at least a bachelor's degree in the geological sciences with at least 36 semester hours of geology, be licensed by the state they wish to work in, undergo peer review, and pay an application fee. A student adjunct certification is also available to those who are majoring in the geological sciences.

More than 30 states require geologists to be registered or licensed. Most of these states require applicants (who have earned a bachelor's degree in the geological sciences) to pass the Fundamentals of Geology exam, a standardized written exam developed by the National Association of State Boards of Geology.

### Other Requirements

In addition to academic training and work experience, geologists who work in the field or in administration must have skills in business administration and in working with other people. Computer modeling, data processing, and effective oral and written communication skills are important, as is the ability to think independently and creatively. Physical stamina is needed for those involved in fieldwork.

## EXPLORING

If this career sounds interesting, try to read as much as possible about geology and geologists. Your best chance for association with geologists and geological work is to join clubs or organizations concerned with such things as rock collecting. Amateur geological groups and local museums also offer opportunities for you to gain exposure to the field of geology.

## EMPLOYERS

Approximately 33,600 geoscientists (including geologists) are employed in the United States. The majority of geologists are employed in private industry. Some work for oil and gas extraction and mining companies, primarily in exploration. The rest work for business services, environmental and geotechnical consulting firms, or are self-employed as consultants to industry and government. The federal government employs geologists in the Department of the Interior (in the U.S. Geological Survey and the Bureau of Reclamation) and in the Departments of Defense, Agriculture, and Commerce. Geologists also work for state agencies, nonprofit research organizations, and museums. Many geologists hold faculty positions at colleges and universities and most of these combine their teaching with research.

## STARTING OUT

After completing sufficient educational requirements, preferably a master's degree or doctorate, the geologist may look for work in various areas, including private industry and government. For those who wish to teach at the college level, a doctorate is required. College graduates may also take government civil service examinations or possibly find work on state geological surveys, which are sometimes based on civil service competition.

Geologists often begin their careers in field exploration or as research assistants in laboratories. As they gain experience, they are given more difficult assignments and may be promoted to supervisory positions, such as project leader or program manager.

## ADVANCEMENT

A geologist with a bachelor's degree has little chance of advancing to higher-level positions. Continued formal training and work experience are necessary, especially as competition for these positions grows more intense. A doctorate is essential for most college or university teaching positions and is preferred for much research work.

## EARNINGS

The U.S. Department of Labor reports that the median annual salary for geoscientists was $81,220 in 2009; the top paid 10 percent earned more than $161,260, while the lowest paid 10 percent earned less than $43,140 a year. In the federal government, the average salary for geologists in managerial, supervisory, and nonsupervisory positions was $94,560 a year. Those employed in the oil and gas extraction industries earned $136,270.

Although the petroleum, mineral, and mining industries offer higher salaries, competition for these jobs is stiff and there is less job security than in other areas. In addition, college and university teachers can earn additional income through research, writing, and consulting. Salaries for foreign assignments may be significantly higher than those in the United States.

Benefits for full-time workers include vacation and sick time, health, and sometimes dental, insurance, and pension or 401(k) plans. Self-employed geologists must provide their own benefits.

## WORK ENVIRONMENT

Some geologists spend most of their time in a laboratory or office, working a regular 40-hour week in pleasant conditions; others divide their time between fieldwork and office or laboratory work. Those who work in the field often travel to remote sites by helicopter or four-wheel drive vehicle and cover large areas on foot. They may camp for extended periods of time in primitive conditions with the members of the geological team as their only companions. Exploration geologists often work overseas or in remote areas, and job relocation is not unusual. Marine geologists may spend considerable time at sea.

## OUTLOOK

Employment of geologists is expected to grow faster than the average for all occupations through 2018, according to the *Occupational Outlook Handbook*. Opportunities in the field will be good because a large number of geologists are expected to retire during the next decade and demand for energy resources is expected to increase. Job opportunities will be especially strong for those with a master's degree who are familiar with computer modeling and the global positioning system (GPS). Geologists who are able to speak a foreign language and who are willing to work overseas will also have strong employment prospects. In addition to the oil, gas, and mining industries, geologists will be able to find jobs in environmental monitoring, protection, and reclamation.

## FOR MORE INFORMATION

*Visit the association's Web site for information on careers and membership for college students, as well as answers to frequently asked questions about the field.*
American Association of Petroleum Geologists
1444 South Boulder
Tulsa, OK 74119-3604
Tel: 800-364-2274
http://www.aapg.org

*For information on geoscience careers, contact*
American Geological Institute
4220 King Street
Alexandria, VA 22302-1502
Tel: 703-379-2480
http://www.agiweb.org

*For information on careers and certification, contact*
American Institute of Professional Geologists
12000 North Washington Street, Suite 285

Thornton, CO 80241-3134
Tel: 303-412-6205
E-mail: aipg@aipg.org
http://www.aipg.org

*For career information and profiles of women in geophysics, visit the AWG Web site.*
Association for Women Geoscientists (AWG)
12000 North Washington Street, Suite 285
Thornton, CO 80241-3134
Tel: 303-412-6219
E-mail: office@awg.org
http://www.awg.org

*For information on the position of state geologist and statistics on minerals, groundwater, and other topics, contact*
Association of American State Geologists
http://www.stategeologists.org

*For career information, contact*
Association of Environmental and Engineering Geologists
PO Box 460518
Denver, CO 80246-0518
Tel: 303-757-2926
E-mail: aeg@aegweb.org
http://www.aegweb.org

*For career information and job listings, contact*
Geological Society of America
PO Box 9140
Boulder, CO 80301-9140
Tel: 888-443-4472
E-mail: gsaservice@geosociety.org
http://www.geosociety.org

*For career information, contact*
National Association of Black Geologists and Geophysicists
4212 San Felipe, Suite 420
Houston, TX 77027-2902
E-mail: nabgg_us @ hotmail.com
http://www.nabgg.com

*For information on the Fundamentals of Geology exam, contact*
National Association of State Boards of Geology
PO Box 11591
Columbia, SC 29211-1591
Tel: 803-739-5676
http://www.asbog.org

*For information about sedimentary geology and related disciplines, contact*
Society for Sedimentary Geology
4111 South Darlington, Suite 100
Tulsa, OK 74135-6373
Tel: 800-865-9765
http://www.sepm.org

*For information about economic geology, contact*
Society of Economic Geologists
7811 Shaffer Parkway
Littleton, CO 80127-3732
Tel: 720-981-7882
E-mail: seg@segweb.org
http://www.segweb.org

*For information on career opportunities, contact*
U.S. Geological Survey
12201 Sunrise Valley Drive
Reston, VA 20192-0002
Tel: 888-275-8747
http://www.usgs.gov/education

*For information on geotechnical engineering, contact*
GEOENGINEER
http://www.geoengineer.org

# Geophysicists

## QUICK FACTS

**School Subjects**
Earth science
Physics

**Personal Skills**
Helping/teaching
Technical/scientific

**Work Environment**
Indoors and outdoors
One location with some
travel

**Minimum Education Level**
Bachelor's degree

**Salary Range**
$43,000 to $81,220 to
$161,260+

**Certification or Licensing**
None available

**Outlook**
Faster than the average

**DOT**
024

**GOE**
02.02.01

**NOC**
2113

**O*NET-SOC**
19-2021.00, 19-2012.00,
19-2042.00

## OVERVIEW

*Geophysicists* are concerned with matter and energy and how they interact. They study the physical properties and structure of the earth, from its interior to its upper atmosphere, including land surfaces, subsurfaces, and bodies of water. There are approximately 33,600 geoscientists employed in the United States.

## HISTORY

Geophysics is an important field that combines the sciences of geology and physics. Geology is the study of the history and composition of the earth as recorded by rock formations and fossils. Physics deals with all forms of energy, the properties of matter, and the relationship between energy and matter. The geophysicist is an "earth physicist," one who works with the physical aspects of the earth from its inner core to outer space.

This alliance between the earth and physical sciences is part of the progress that science has made in searching for new understandings of the world. Like the fields of biochemistry, biomathematics, space medicine, and nuclear physics, geophysics combines the knowledge of two disciplines. However, the importance of geophysics goes well beyond abstract theory. Geophysicists apply their knowledge to such practical problems as predicting earthquakes and tsunamis, locating raw materials and sources of power, and evaluating sites for power plants.

## Facts About Natural Gas

- Natural gas is odorless, colorless, and tasteless.
- More than 50 percent of U.S. homes are heated by natural gas.
- Natural gas is used to create glass, paper, steel, brick, paint, antifreeze, dyes, medicines, propane, clothing, electricity, fertilizer, plastics, photographic film, and explosives.
- Natural gas is used by the following sectors: industrial, 31 percent; electric power, 31 percent; residential, 23 percent; commercial, 15 percent.
- Natural gas is the cleanest burning fossil fuel.

Sources: Energy Information Administration, *Natural Gas Annual 2008*

## THE JOB

Geophysicists use the principles and techniques of geology, physics, chemistry, mathematics, and engineering to perform tests and conduct research on the surface, atmosphere, waters, and solid bodies of the earth. They study seismic, gravitational, electrical, thermal, and magnetic phenomena to determine the structure and composition of the earth, as well as the forces causing movement and warping of the surface.

Many geophysicists are involved in fieldwork, where they engage in exploration and prospecting. Others work in laboratories, where research activities are the main focus. They use computer modeling software to develop and test their hypotheses. Photogrammetry, geographic information systems (GIS), and remote sensing technology is often used to gather geophysical data. In general, their instruments are highly complex and designed to take very precise measurements. Most geophysicists specialize in one of the following areas.

*Geodesists* measure the shape and size of the earth to determine fixed points, positions, and elevations on or near the earth's surface. Using the gravimeter, they perform surveys to measure minute variations in the earth's gravitational field. They also collect data that is useful in learning more about the weight, size, and mass of the earth. Geodesists are active in tracking satellites orbiting in outer space.

*Geomagnetists* use the magnetometer to measure variations in the earth's magnetic field from magnetic observatories and stations.

They are also concerned with conditions affecting radio signals, solar phenomena, and many other aspects of space exploration. The data gathered can be most helpful in working with problems in radio and television transmission, telegraphy, navigation, mapping, and space exploration and space science.

*Applied geophysicists* use data gathered from the air, ground, and ocean floor, as well as computers, to analyze the earth's crust. They look for oil and mineral deposits and try to find sites for the safe disposal of hazardous wastes.

*Exploration geophysicists,* sometimes called *geophysical prospectors,* use seismic techniques to look for possible oil and gas deposits on land and in oceans. They may use sonar equipment to send sound waves deep into the earth or beneath the ocean surface. The resulting echo helps them estimate if an oil deposit lies hidden in the area.

*Hydrologists* are concerned with the surface and underground waters in the land areas of the earth. They map and chart the flow and the disposition of sediments, measure changes in water volume, and collect data on the form and intensity of precipitation, as well as on the disposition of water through evaporation and ground absorption. The information that the hydrologist collects is applied to problems in flood control, crop production, soil and water conservation, irrigation, and inland water projects. Some hydrologists study glaciers and their sedimentation.

*Marine geophysicists* are geophysicists who apply their training to the study of our world's oceans. They conduct research on how matter and energy affect the ocean. In particular, they study the makeup of the earth's surface and waters and how geophysical phenomena such as earthquakes, tsunamis, and underwater volcanoes and hydrothermal systems change them.

*Seismologists* use sound waves to study the earth's interior structure. They specialize in the study of earthquakes. With the aid of the seismogram and other instruments that record the location of earthquakes and the vibrations they cause, seismologists examine active fault lines and areas where earthquakes have occurred. They are often members of field teams whose purpose is to examine and evaluate possible building or construction sites. They also may explore for oil and minerals. In recent years, seismologists have contributed to the selection of missile launching sites. Seismologists who study the ocean floor can pinpoint areas where earthquakes may occur. Earthquakes can sometimes cause tsunamis, which can kill or injure people in regions far from the earthquake site. Seismologists also try to answer questions such as: What does the deep interior of the earth look like? and What is the role of upper earth mantle structures in tectonic plate interactions?

*Tectonophysicists* study the structure of mountains and ocean basins, the properties of the earth's crust, and the physical forces and processes that cause movements and changes in the structure of the earth. A great deal of their work is research, and their findings are helpful in locating oil and mineral deposits.

*Volcanologists* study volcanoes, their location, and their activity. They are concerned with their origins and the phenomena of their processes.

*Planetologists* use data from artificial satellites and astronauts' equipment to study the makeup and atmosphere of the planets, the moon, and other bodies in our solar system. Recent advances in this field have greatly increased our knowledge of Jupiter, Saturn, and their satellites.

# REQUIREMENTS

## High School

A strong interest in the physical and earth sciences is essential for this field. You should take basic courses in earth science, physics, chemistry, and at least four years of mathematics. Advanced placement work in any of the mathematics and sciences is also helpful. Other recommended courses include mechanical drawing, shop, social studies, English, and computer science.

## Postsecondary Training

A bachelor's degree in geophysics is required for most entry-level positions. Physics, mathematics, and chemistry majors can locate positions in geophysics, but some work in geology is highly desirable and often required, especially for certain government positions.

Graduate work at the master's or doctoral level is required for research, college teaching, and positions of a policy-making or policy-interpreting nature in private or government employment.

Many colleges and universities offer a bachelor's degree in geophysics, and a growing number of these institutions also award advanced degrees. An undergraduate major in geophysics is not usually required for entrance into a graduate program.

## Other Requirements

If you seek employment in the federal government, you will have to take a civil service examination and be able to meet other specified requirements.

You should also possess a strong aptitude in mathematics and science, particularly the physical and earth sciences, and an interest in observing nature, performing experiments, and studying the physical environment. Because geophysicists frequently spend time outdoors, you should enjoy outdoor activities such as hiking and camping.

## EXPLORING

You can explore various aspects of this field by taking earth and physical science courses. Units of study dealing with electricity, rocks and minerals, metals and metallurgy, the universe and space, and weather and climate may offer you an opportunity for further learning about the field. Hobbies that deal with radio, electronics, and rock or map collecting also offer opportunities to learn about the basic principles involved in geophysics.

Some colleges and universities have a student chapter of the Society of Exploration Geophysicists that you can join. Employment as an aide or helper with a geophysical field party may be available during the summer months and provide you with the opportunity to study the physical environment and interact with geophysicists.

## EMPLOYERS

Approximately 33,600 geoscientists (including geophysicists) are employed in the United States. Geophysicists are employed primarily by the petroleum industry, mining companies, exploration and consulting firms, and research institutions. A few geophysicists work as consultants, offering their services on a fee or contract basis. Many work for the federal government, mainly the National Geodetic Survey, the U.S. Geological Survey, and the Naval Oceanographic Office. Other geophysicists pursue teaching careers.

## STARTING OUT

Most college career services offices are prepared to help students locate positions in business, industry, and government agencies. Other job contacts can be made through professors, friends, and relatives. Some companies visit college campuses in the spring of each year to interview candidates who are interested in positions as geophysicists. College career services offices can usually provide helpful information on job opportunities in the field of geophysics.

Additionally, some associations, such as the Seismological Society of America, offer job listings at their Web sites.

# ADVANCEMENT

If employed by a private firm, a new employee with only a bachelor's degree will probably have an on-the-job training period. As a company trainee, the beginning geophysicist may be assigned to a number of different jobs. On a field party, the trainee will probably work with a junior geophysicist, which in many companies is the level of assignment received after the training has ended.

From a junior geophysicist, advancement is usually to intermediate geophysicist, and eventually to geophysicist. From this point, one can transfer to research positions or, if the geophysicist remains in fieldwork, to *party chief*.

The party chief coordinates the work of people in a crew, including trainees; junior, intermediate, and full geophysicists; surveyors; observers; drillers; shooters; and aides. Advancement with the company may eventually lead to supervisory and management positions.

Geophysicists can often transfer to other jobs in the fields of geology, physics, and engineering, depending on their qualifications and experience.

# EARNINGS

The salaries of geophysicists are comparable to the earnings of those in other scientific professions. According to the U.S. Department of Labor, geoscientists (which includes geologists, geophysicists, and oceanographers) earned an average annual salary of $81,220 in 2009. The lowest paid 10 percent earned less than $43,140 per year, while the highest paid 10 percent earned more than $161,260 annually. In 2009, the average salary for a geophysicist working in the oil and gas extraction industry was $136,270. Those employed by the federal government earned $94,560. Positions in colleges and universities offer annual salaries ranging from about $43,000 for instructors to $133,000 for full professors. Salaries depend upon experience, education, and professional rank. Faculty members may teach in summer school for additional compensation and also engage in writing, consulting, and research for government, industry, or business.

Additional compensation is awarded to geophysicists who are required to live outside the United States.

Both the federal government and private industry provide additional benefits, including vacations, retirement pensions, health and life insurance, and sick leave benefits.

## WORK ENVIRONMENT

Geophysicists employed in laboratories or offices generally work a regular 40-hour week under typical office conditions. Field geophysicists work under a variety of conditions and often the hours are irregular. They are outdoors much of the time in all kinds of weather. The work requires carrying small tools and equipment and occasionally some heavy lifting. The field geophysicist is often required to travel and work in isolated areas. Volcanologists, for example, may face dangerous conditions when visiting and gathering data near an erupting volcano.

## OUTLOOK

Employment of geophysicists is expected to grow faster than the average for all occupations through 2018, according to the *Occupational Outlook Handbook*. The total number of graduates with degrees in the geophysical sciences is expected to remain small and insufficient to meet the moderate increase in industry job openings. Those with advanced degrees, experience in the field, and a willingness to travel will have the best employment opportunities.

The petroleum industry, the largest employer of geophysicists, has increased its exploration activities, and more geophysicists will be needed to locate less-accessible fuel and mineral deposits and to do research on such problems as radioactivity, cosmic and solar radiation, and the use of geothermal energy to generate electricity. The petroleum industry is also expected to expand operations overseas, which may create new jobs for those who are willing to travel.

More geophysicists will be needed to study water conservation and flood control and to assist in space science projects. The growing need to find new sources of energy will undoubtedly make the work of geophysicists more important and more challenging during the next few decades.

## FOR MORE INFORMATION

*For information on geoscience careers, contact*
American Geological Institute
4220 King Street
Alexandria, VA 22302-1502
Tel: 703-379-2480
http://www.agiweb.org

*For information on local meetings, publications, job opportunities, and science news, contact*

American Geophysical Union
2000 Florida Avenue, NW
Washington, DC 20009-1277
Tel: 800-966-2481
http://www.agu.org

*For career information and profiles of women in geophysics, visit the AWG Web site.*
Association for Women Geoscientists (AWG)
12000 North Washington Street, Suite 285
Thornton, CO 80241-3134
Tel: 303-412-6219
E-mail: office@awg.org
http://www.awg.org

*For information on careers and the society's specialty divisions, contact*
Geological Society of America
PO Box 9140
Boulder, CO 80301-9140
Tel: 888-443-4472
E-mail: gsaservice@geosociety.org
http://www.geosociety.org

*For an overview of remote sensing, contact*
Geoscience and Remote Sensing Society
Institute of Electrical and Electronics Engineers
445 Hoes Lane
Piscataway, NJ 08854-4141
E-mail: info@grss-ieee.org
http://www.grss-ieee.org

*For career information, contact*
National Association of Black Geologists and Geophysicists
4212 San Felipe, Suite 420
Houston, TX 77027-2902
E-mail: nabgg_us @ hotmail.com
http://www.nabgg.com

*For information about marine geophysics and oceanography, contact*
National Oceanic and Atmospheric Administration
c/o U.S. Department of Commerce

1401 Constitution Avenue, NW, Room 5128
Washington, DC 20230-0001
http://www.noaa.gov

*For career information and job listings, contact*
**Seismological Society of America**
201 Plaza Professional Building
El Cerrito, CA 94530
Tel: 510-525-5474
E-mail: info@seismosoc.org
http://www.seismosoc.org

*For information on careers in geophysics and a virtual museum,
visit the society's Web site.*
**Society of Exploration Geophysicists**
PO Box 702740
Tulsa, OK 74170-2740
Tel: 918-497-5500
http://www.seg.org

*To read the online publication* Become a Geophysicist . . . A What?,
*visit*
**U.S. Geological Survey**
http://education.usgs.gov or
http://earthquake.usgs.gov/learn/kids/become.php

*To learn more about coastal and marine geology, visit*
**U.S. Geological Survey: Coastal and Marine Geology Program**
http://marine.usgs.gov

# Line Installers and Cable Splicers

## OVERVIEW

*Line installers and cable splicers* construct, maintain, and repair the vast network of wires and cables that transmit electric power and voice, video, and Internet communications services to commercial and residential customers. Line construction and cable splicing is a vital part of the communications system. Workers are involved in linking electricity between generation plants and homes and other buildings; providing landline, cellular, and Internet-based phone service to customers; and bringing cable television stations and Internet connections to residences and other locations. There are approximately 284,900 line installers and cable splicers working in the United States.

## HISTORY

The occupation of line installers and cable splicers is related to major developments in electromagnetic technology since the late 19th century. The roots of this technology are traced to 1831, when Michael Faraday discovered electric induction. In the late 1880s came the invention and patents for the incandescent lamp, and by the turn of the century electric lighting was a common phenomenon throughout urban areas.

The generation of electricity took on further commercial significance as the telecommunications industry was born after Alexander Graham Bell's patent of the telephone in 1876. During the first quarter of the 20th century, the electronics industry focused on communications and broadcast entertainment. As the need developed for more and more telephone lines to connect distant points throughout the country, line installers and cable splicers were trained and employed to construct and maintain these lines.

After World War II, the television started to become a common addition in homes around the country. In the 1950s, cable television systems were designed for better reception of network broadcasts in remote areas, and by the 1970s such systems were becoming familiar to residential viewers. Extensive construction of cable systems was begun during the 1980s to provide service to people in all geographic regions. In the 1990s, many cable television companies started to use fiber optics for new systems and to upgrade existing systems. Fiber optic technology increases network capacity, or bandwidth, thus allowing more channels to subscribers, and allows for higher-quality sound and video reception.

Today, telecommunications companies are using advanced technologies to modernize their equipment and build new telecommunications systems that allow voice, data, and video transmissions over the same lines. This is expected to generate increased construction activity during the 21st century; however, it is uncertain how many jobs will be generated from the expected boom, as much of the new equipment is maintenance free and requires far fewer workers in terms of repairs and upkeep.

## THE JOB

In the installation of new telecommunications and electric power lines, workers use power-driven machinery to first dig holes and erect the poles or towers that are used to support the cables. (In some areas, lines must be buried underground, and in these cases installers use power-driven equipment to dig and to place the cables in underground conduits.) These line installers, also called *outside plant technicians* and *construction line workers,* climb the poles using metal rungs (or they use truck-mounted work platforms) and install the necessary equipment and cables. Once they have built the infrastructure, line installers string cable along towers and poles or underground through tunnels and trenches. In some cases, installers must attach other wires to the customer's premises in order to connect the customer with the outside line.

Installers who work with telecommunications lines usually leave the ends of the wires free for cable splicers to connect afterward; installers who work with electric power lines usually do the splicing of the wires themselves. For work on electric power lines, insulators must first be set into the poles before cables are attached. To join sections of power line and to conduct transformers and electrical accessories, line installers splice, solder, and insulate the conductors

Linemen install power lines on a new pole. *(Greg Wahl-Stephens, AP Photo)*

and related wiring. In some cases, line installers must attach other equipment—such as transformers, circuit breakers, and devices that deter lightning—to the line poles.

After line installers have completed the installation of underground conduits or poles, wires, and cables, cable splicers complete the line connections; they also rearrange wires when lines are changed. To join the individual wires within the cable, splicers must cut the lead sheath and insulation from the cables. They then test or phase out each conductor to identify corresponding conductors in adjoining cable sections according to electrical diagrams and specifications. At each splice, they either wrap insulation around the wires and seal the joint with a lead sleeve or cover the splice with some other type of closure. Sometimes they fill the sheathing with pressurized air so that leaks can be located and repaired.

In the past, copper was the material of choice for cables. To allow for the demands of high-speed, high-definition transmissions, many telecommunications companies are installing fiber optic cables. Fiber optic cables are hair-thin strands of glass or plastic that transmit signals more efficiently than do copper wires. For work with fiber optic cable, splicing is performed in workshop vans located near the splice area. Splicers of copper cables do their work on aerial platforms, down in manholes, in basements, or in underground vaults where the cables are located.

Preventive maintenance and repair work occupy major portions of the line installer's and cable splicer's time. When wires or cables break or poles are knocked down, workers are sent immediately to make emergency repairs. Such repair work is usually necessary after the occurrence of such disasters as storms and earthquakes. The *line crew supervisor* is notified when there is a break in a line and is directed to the trouble spot by workers who keep a check on the condition of all lines in given areas. During the course of routine periodic inspection, the line installer also makes minor repairs and line changes. Workers often use electric and gas pressure tests to detect possible trouble.

Hybrid fiber/coax systems requires far less maintenance than traditional copper-based networks. As a result, line installers and cable splicers will spend significantly less time repairing broken wires and cables as hybrid fiber/coax systems continue to become more prevalent. As the cost of fiber cables decreases and becomes more in line with the costs of copper cables, more telecommunications companies will make the switch. Included in this occupation are many specialists, such as the following: section line maintainers, tower line repairers, line construction checkers, tower erectors, and cable testers. Other types of related workers include troubleshooters, test desk trouble locators, steel-post installers, radio interference investigators, and electric power line examiners.

## REQUIREMENTS

### High School
You will need math courses to prepare for the technical nature of this career. While in high school you should also take any shop classes that will teach you the principles of electricity and how to work with it. In addition, you will benefit from taking any classes that deal with electricity at a vocational or technical college in your area. Other high school shop classes, such as machinery, will give you the opportunity to work with tools and improve your hand–eye coordination. Science classes that involve lab work will also be beneficial. Take computer classes so that you will be able to use this tool in your professional life. Because you may be frequently interacting with customers, take English, speech, and other courses that will help you develop communication skills.

### Postsecondary Training
Many companies prefer to hire applicants with a high school diploma or the equivalent. Although specific educational courses are not required, you'll need certain qualifications. It is helpful to have some knowledge of the basic principles of electricity and the proce-

dures involved in line installation; such information can be obtained through attending technical programs or having been a member of the armed forces. Many employers prefer to hire applicants who have received some technical training or completed a trade school or technical program that offers certification classes in technology such as fiber optics. Training can also be obtained through special classes offered through trade associations. The Society of Cable Telecommunications Engineers (SCTE) offers seminars that provide hands-on, technical training.

In many companies, entry-level employees must complete a formal apprenticeship program combining classroom instruction with supervised on-the-job training. These programs often last several years and are administered by both the employer and the union representing the employees. The programs may involve computer-assisted instruction as well as hands-on experience with simulated environments. Other employers provide on-the-job training.

### Certification or Licensing

Though not a requirement for employment, certification demonstrates to employers that a line installer has achieved a certain level of technical training and has been proven qualified to perform certain functions. The SCTE offers several certification designations to applicants who show technical knowledge and practical skills by passing both multiple-choice and essay-based examinations. (Contact information for the SCTE is listed at the end of this article.)

Employers may also give preemployment tests to applicants to determine verbal, mechanical, and mathematical aptitudes; some employers test applicants for such physical qualifications as stamina, balance, coordination, and strength. Workers who drive a company vehicle need a driver's license and a good driving record.

Unions represent many workers, and union membership may be required. Two unions that represent many line installers and cable splicers are the International Brotherhood of Electrical Workers (IBEW) and the Communications Workers of America (CWA).

### Other Requirements

You will need manual dexterity and to be in good physical shape. Much of your work will involve climbing poles and ladders, so you will need to feel comfortable with heights. You also need to be strong in order to carry heavy equipment up poles and ladders. Also, because lines and cables are color coded, you should have the ability to distinguish such colors. You may have extensive contact with the public and need to be polite and courteous.

## EXPLORING

In high school or vocational school, you can test your ability and interest in the occupations of line installer and cable splicer through courses in mathematics, electrical applications, and machine shop. Hobbies that involve knowledge of and experience with electricity also provide valuable practical experience. To observe line installers and cable splicers at work, it may be possible to have a school counselor arrange a field trip by calling the public relations office of the local telephone or cable television company.

Direct training and experience in telephone work may be gained in the armed forces. Frequently, those who have received such training are given preference for job openings and may be hired in positions above the entry level.

## EMPLOYERS

There are approximately 284,900 line installers and cable splicers working in the United States. About 60 percent work in the telecommunications industry, with the other 40 percent employed in the electrical power industry. Some installers also work for the freelance construction companies that contract with telecommunications and electric companies.

## STARTING OUT

Those who meet the basic requirements and are interested in becoming either a line installer or a cable splicer may inquire about job openings by directly contacting the personnel offices of local telecommunications and utility companies.

Those enrolled in a trade school or technical institute may be able to find out about job openings through their schools' career services office. Occasionally, employers will contact teachers and program administrators, so it is helpful to check with them also. Some positions are advertised through classified advertisements in the newspaper or at the Web sites of professional associations. Because many line installers are members of unions such as the CWA and the IBEW, job seekers can contact their local offices for job leads and assistance or visit these unions' Web sites.

# ADVANCEMENT

Entry-level line installers are generally hired as helpers, trainees, or ground workers; cable splicers tend to work their way up from the position of line installer.

After successfully completing an on-the-job training program, the employee will be assigned either as a line crewmember under the guidance of a line supervisor or as a cable splicer's helper under the guidance of experienced splicers. Cable splicers' helpers advance to positions of qualified cable splicers after three to four years of working experience.

Both the line installer and the cable splicer must continue to receive training throughout their careers, not only to qualify for advancement but also to keep up with the technological changes that occur in the industry. Usually it takes line installers about six years to reach top pay for their job; top pay for cable splicers is earned after about five to seven years of work experience.

In companies represented by unions, opportunities for advancement may be based on seniority. Workers who demonstrate technical expertise in addition to certain personal characteristics, such as good judgment, planning skills, and the ability to deal with people, may progress to foremen or line crew supervisors.

# EARNINGS

For line installers and cable splicers, earnings vary according to different regions of the country, and as with most occupations, work experience and length of service determine advances in scale. The U.S. Department of Labor (DOL) reports that electrical power line installers and repairs earned median salaries of $56,670 in 2009. Salaries ranged from less than $32,170 to $80,310 or more. Telecommunications line installers and repairers earned salaries that ranged from less than $26,520 to $70,230 or more. When emergencies arise and overtime is necessary during unscheduled hours, workers are guaranteed a minimum rate of pay that is higher than their regular rate.

Beginning workers and those with only a few years of experience make significantly less than more experienced workers. As mentioned earlier, the turnover rate in these occupations is low; therefore, many workers are in the higher wage categories. Also, cable splicers who work with fiber optics tend to earn more than those who work with copper cables.

Telecommunications and electric companies often provide workers with many benefits. Although benefits vary from company to company, in general, most workers receive paid holidays, vacations, and sick leaves. In addition, most companies offer medical, dental, and life insurance plans. Some companies offer pension plans.

## WORK ENVIRONMENT

Most line installers and cable splicers work standard 40-hour weeks, though evening and weekend work is not unusual. For example, line installers and cable splicers who work for construction companies may need to schedule their work around contractors' activities and then be required to rush to complete a job on schedule. Shift work, such as four 10-hour days or working Tuesday through Saturday, is common for many workers. Most workers earn extra pay for any work over 40 hours a week.

Some workers are on call 24 hours a day and need to be available for emergencies. Both occupations require that workers perform their jobs outdoors, often in severe weather conditions when emergency repairs are needed. Construction line installers usually work in crews of two to five persons, with a supervisor directing the work of several of these crews. Work may involve extensive travel, including overnight trips during emergencies to distant locations.

There is a great deal of climbing involved in these occupations, and some underground work must be done in stooped and cramped conditions. Cable splicers sometimes perform their work on board a marine craft if they are employed with an underwater cable crew.

The work can be physically demanding and poses significant risk of injury from shocks or falls. The hazards of this work have been greatly reduced, though, by concerted efforts to establish safety standards. Such efforts have been put forward by the telecommunications companies, utility companies, and appropriate labor unions.

## OUTLOOK

The DOL anticipates that employment for line installers and cable splicers will experience little change through 2018. Despite this prediction, there should be many opportunities for line installers and cable splicers—especially in the electric power industry. An expected wave of retirements, the need for preventive maintenance on telecommunications and electrical infrastructure, and increasing demand for electricity and telecommunications services from a growing population will create a need for workers in the field.

# FOR MORE INFORMATION

*For job listings and general information on the power industry, contact*
American Public Power Association
1875 Connecticut Avenue, NW, Suite 1200
Washington, DC 20009-5715
Tel: 800-515-2772
http://www.publicpower.org

*For information about union representation, contact the following organizations:*
Communications Workers of America
501 Third Street, NW
Washington, DC 20001-2797
Tel: 202-434-1100
http://www.cwa-union.org

International Brotherhood of Electrical Workers
900 Seventh Street, NW
Washington, DC 20001-3886
Tel: 202-833-7000
http://www.ibew.org

*To read* Electricity 101, *visit the following Web site:*
Edison Electric Institute
701 Pennsylvania Avenue, NW
Washington, DC 20004-2696
Tel: 202-508-5000
http://www.eei.org

*For information on careers and the cable industry, contact*
National Cable and Telecommunications Association
25 Massachusetts Avenue, NW, Suite 100
Washington, DC 20001-1434
Tel: 202-222-2300
http://www.ncta.com

*For information on educational training, contact*
National Coalition for Telecommunications Education and
   Learning
6021 South Syracuse Way, Suite 213
Greenwood Village, CO 80111-4747
http://www.nactel.org

*For information on training seminars and certification, contact*
Society of Cable Telecommunications Engineers
140 Philips Road
Exton, PA 19341-1318
Tel: 800-542-5040
E-mail: scte@scte.org
http://www.scte.org

*For information about career opportunities for women, contact*
Women in Cable Telecommunications
14555 Avion Parkway, Suite 250
Chantilly, VA 20151-1117
Tel: 703-234-9810
http://www.wict.org

# Mining Engineers

## OVERVIEW

*Mining engineers* deal with the exploration, location, and planning for removal of minerals and mineral deposits from the earth. These include metals (iron, copper), nonmetallic minerals (limestone, gypsum), and coal. Mining engineers conduct preliminary surveys of mineral deposits and examine them to ascertain whether they can be extracted efficiently and economically, using either underground or surface mining methods. They plan and design the development of mine shafts and tunnels, devise means of extracting minerals, and select the methods to be used in transporting the minerals to the surface. They supervise all mining operations and are responsible for mine safety. Mining engineers normally specialize in design, research and development, or production. *Mining equipment engineers* may specialize in design, research, testing, or sales of equipment and services. Mines also require *safety engineers*.

There are approximately 7,100 mining and geological engineers employed in the United States.

## QUICK FACTS

**School Subjects**
Earth science
Mathematics

**Personal Skills**
Mechanical/manipulative
Technical/scientific

**Work Environment**
Indoors and outdoors
Primarily multiple locations

**Minimum Education Level**
Bachelor's degree

**Salary Range**
$48,400 to $79,440 to
$119,300+

**Certification or Licensing**
Required

**Outlook**
Faster than the average

**DOT**
010

**GOE**
02.07.02

**NOC**
2143

**O*NET-SOC**
17-2151.00

## HISTORY

The development of mining technology stretches back some 50,000 years to the period when people began digging pits and stripping surface cover in search of stone and flint for tools. Between 8000 and 3000 B.C., the search for quality flint led people to sink shafts and drive galleries into limestone deposits.

By about 1300 B.C., the Egyptians and other Near Eastern peoples were mining copper and gold by driving adits (near-horizontal entry tunnels) into hillsides, then sinking inclined shafts from which they drove extensive galleries. They supported the gallery roofs with pillars of uncut ore or wooden props.

Providing adequate ventilation posed a difficult problem in ancient underground mines. Because of the small dimensions of the passageways, air circulated poorly. All methods of ventilating the mines relied on the natural circulation of air by draft and convection. To assist this process, ancient engineers carefully calculated the number, location, and depth of the shafts. At the great Greek mining complex of Laurion, they sank shafts in pairs and drove parallel galleries from them with frequent crosscuts between galleries to assist airflow. Lighting a fire in one shaft caused a downdraft in the other.

Ancient Roman engineers made further advances in the mining techniques of the Greeks and Egyptians. They mined more ambitiously than the Greeks, sometimes exploiting as many as four levels by means of deep connecting shafts. Careful planning enabled them to drive complicated networks of exploratory galleries at various depths. Buckets of rock and ore could be hoisted up the main shaft by means of a windlass. Unlike the Greeks and Egyptians, the Romans often worked mines far below groundwater level. Engineers overcame the danger of flooding to some extent by developing effective, if expensive, drainage methods and machinery. Where terrain allowed, they devised an elaborate system of crosscuts to channel off the water. In addition, they adapted Archimedean screws—originally used for crop irrigation—to drain mine workings. A series of inclined screws, each emptying water into a tub emptied by a screw above it, could raise a considerable amount of water in a short time. It took only one man to rotate each screw, which made it perhaps the most efficient application of labor until engineers discovered the advantage of cutting halls large enough for an animal to rotate the screw. By the first century A.D., the Romans had designed water wheels, which greatly increased the height to which water could be raised in mines.

Mining engineering advanced little from Roman times until the 11th century. From this period on, however, basic mining operations such as drainage, ventilation, and hoisting underwent increasing mechanization. In his book *De Re Metallica* (1556), the German scholar Georgius Agricola presented a detailed description of the devices and practices mining engineers had developed since ancient times. Drainage pumps in particular grew more and more sophisticated. One pump sucked water from mines by the movement of water-wheel-driven pistons.

As mines went deeper, technological problems required new engineering solutions. During the 18th century, engineers developed cheap, reliable steam-powered pumps to raise water in mines. Steam-powered windlasses also came into use. In the 1800s, engineers invented power drills for making shot holes for rock-breaking explosives. This greatly increased the capability to mine hard rock. In coal mines, revolving-wheel cutters—powered by steam, then by compressed air, then by electricity—relieved miners from the dangerous task of undercutting coal seams by hand. As late as the mid-19th century, ore was still being pushed or hauled through mines by people and animals. After 1900, however, electric locomotives, conveyor belts, and large-capacity rubber-tired vehicles came into wide use so that haulage could keep pace with mechanized ore breaking. The development of large, powerful machines also made possible the removal of vast amounts of material from open-pit mines.

## THE JOB

Before the decision is made to mine a newly discovered mineral deposit, mining engineers must go through successive stages of information gathering, evaluation, and planning. As long as they judge the project to be economically viable, they proceed to the next stage. Review and planning for a major mining project may take a decade or longer and may cost many millions of dollars.

A chief mining engineer studies rocks at a freshly blasted area in a mine. *(Michael Penn, The Juneau Empire/AP Photo)*

First mining engineers try to get a general idea of the deposit's potential. They accomplish this by reviewing geological data, product marketing information, and government requirements for permits, public hearings, and environmental protection. Based on this review, they prepare rough cost estimates and economic analyses. If it appears possible to mine the deposit at a competitive price with an acceptable return on investment, mining engineers undertake a more detailed review.

Meanwhile, geologists continue to explore the mineral deposit in order to ascertain its dimensions and character. Once the deposit has been reasonably well defined, mining engineers estimate the percentage of the deposit that can be profitably extracted. This estimate, which takes into account the ore's grade (value) and tonnage (volume and density), constitutes the minable ore reserve. It provides mining engineers with enough specific information to refine their economic appraisal and justify further analysis.

At this stage, engineers begin the process of selecting the most suitable mining method—one that will yield the largest profit consistent with safety and efficient ore extraction. In considering the adaptability of mining methods to the deposit, they rely heavily on rock mechanics and geologic data. Measurements of the stresses, strains, and displacements in the rock surrounding the ore body help engineers predict roof-support requirements and settling of rock masses during excavation. Evaluation of the deposit's geologic features (such as the dimensions, inclination, strength, and physical character of the ore and overlying rock) enables engineers to place mine openings in stable rock, avoid underground water, and plan overall excavation procedures. If the evaluation calls for surface mining, engineers must decide where to dig the pits and where to put the rock and soil removed during mining.

Having estimated the ore reserve, chosen a mining method, and begun mine planning, engineers can determine daily (or yearly) mine output tonnage in light of product demand. They also select equipment and help plan and size the mine's plant, support, ore-processing, and shipping facilities.

For underground mining, mining engineers must determine the number and location of mine shafts, tunnels, and main extraction openings. They must also determine the size, number, kind, and layout of the various pieces of equipment. If the project continues to appear economically viable, construction begins.

As actual mine-making proceeds, mining engineers supervise operations. They train crews of workers and supervisors. The stress fields around the mine workings change as the mine expands.

Engineers and engineering technicians must inspect the roof of underground cavities to ensure that it continues to have adequate support. Engineers must also continually monitor the quality of air in the mine to ensure proper ventilation. In addition, mining engineers inspect and repair mining equipment. Some mining engineers help plan ways of restoring or reclaiming the land around mine sites so that it can be used for other purposes.

Some mining engineers specialize in designing equipment used to excavate and operate mines. This equipment typically includes ventilation systems, earth- and rock-moving conveyors, and underground railroads and elevators. Engineers also design the equipment that chips and cuts rock and coal. Others select and determine the placement of explosives used to blast ore deposits.

Mining engineers also work for firms that sell mining supplies and equipment. Experienced mining engineers teach in colleges and universities and serve as independent consultants to industry and government.

## REQUIREMENTS

### High School

To meet the standards set by most engineering colleges, high school students should take as much math and science as possible. Minimum course work includes elementary and intermediate algebra, plane geometry, trigonometry, chemistry, and physics. Courses in solid geometry, advanced algebra, and basic computer functions are highly recommended. In addition, many engineering colleges require three years of English (preferably emphasizing composition and public speaking) and social science (especially economics and history). Course work in foreign languages also is helpful, because many engineers work overseas.

### Postsecondary Training

A bachelor's degree in engineering, preferably with a major in mining engineering, from an accredited engineering program is the minimum requirement for beginning mining engineering jobs. The organization that accredits engineering programs in the United States is the Accreditation Board for Engineering and Technology (ABET). ABET-accredited mining engineering programs assure students that their education will prepare them for professional practice and graduate study.

In a typical undergraduate engineering program, students spend the first two years studying basic sciences, such as mathematics, physics, and chemistry, as well as introductory engineering. Students must also study such subjects as economics, foreign languages, history, management, and writing. These courses equip students with skills they will need in their future work as engineers. The remaining years of college are devoted mostly to engineering courses, usually with a concentration in mining engineering. Engineering programs can last from four to six years. Those that require five to six years to complete may award a master's degree or provide a cooperative engineering education program. Cooperative programs allow students to combine classroom education and practical work experience with a participating mining company or engineering firm.

After completing their formal studies and landing a job, many mining engineers continue their education. They take courses, attend workshops, and read professional journals in order to keep up with developments in their field. Continuing education also enables them to acquire expertise in new technical areas. Some mining engineers pursue advanced degrees. A graduate degree is needed for most teaching and research positions and for many management positions. Some mining engineers pursue graduate study in engineering, business, or law.

Visit the Society for Mining, Metallurgy, and Exploration's Web site, http://www.smenet.org, for a list of postsecondary mining engineering programs.

## Certification or Licensing

Regardless of their educational credentials, mining engineers normally must obtain professional certification in the states in which they work. Professional registration is mandatory for mining engineers whose work may affect life, health, or property or who offer their services to the public. Registration generally requires a degree from an ABET-accredited engineering program, four years of relevant work experience, and passing a state examination. For more information on licensing and examination requirements, visit the National Council of Examiners for Engineering and Surveying's Web site, http://www.ncees.org.

## Other Requirements

Certain characteristics help qualify a person for a career in mining engineering. These include the judgment to adapt knowledge to practical purposes, the imagination and analytical skill to solve problems, the ability to remain calm under pressure, and the capacity to predict the performance and cost of new processes or devices.

Mining engineers must also be able to communicate effectively, work as part of a team, and supervise other workers.

## EXPLORING

To learn about the profession of mining engineering, you may find it helpful to talk with science teachers and school counselors and with people employed in the minerals industry. You might also wish to read more about the industry and its engineers.

Companies and government agencies that employ graduates of mining engineering programs also hire undergraduates as part of a cooperative engineering education program. Students often enter such programs the summer preceding their junior year, after they have taken a certain number of engineering courses. They normally alternate terms of on-campus study and terms of work at the employer's facilities.

On the job, students assume the role of a junior mining engineer. They report to an experienced engineer, who acts as their supervisor and counselor. He or she assigns them work within their capabilities, evaluates their performance, and advises them as though they were permanent employees. Students have ample opportunity to interact with a diverse group of engineers and managers and to ask them about their work, their company, and mining engineering in general. Participation in the actual practice of the profession can help students assess their own aptitudes and interests and decide which courses will be most useful to them during the remainder of their engineering program.

## EMPLOYERS

There are approximately 7,100 mining and geological engineers employed in the United States. Nearly 50 percent work in the mining industry itself; the others work for government agencies, engineering consulting firms, and in academia.

## STARTING OUT

Beginning mining engineers generally perform routine tasks under the supervision of experienced engineers. Some mining companies provide starting engineers with in-house training. As engineers gain knowledge and experience, they receive increasingly difficult assignments along with greater independence to develop designs, solve problems, and make decisions.

## ADVANCEMENT

Mining engineers may become directors of specific mining projects. Some head research projects. Mining engineers may go on to work as technical specialists or to supervise a team of engineers and technicians. Some eventually manage their mining company's engineering department or enter other managerial, management support, or sales positions.

## EARNINGS

The U.S. Department of Labor (DOL) reports that median annual earnings of mining and geological engineers were $79,440 in 2009. Salaries ranged from less than $48,400 to $119,300 or more. The DOL reports the following mean annual earning for mining engineers by industry: oil and gas extraction, $97,140; metal ore mining, $78,780; architectural, engineering, and related services, $77,210; and coal mining, $76,580.

According to a 2009 salary survey by the National Association of Colleges and Employers, new graduates with bachelor's degrees in mining and mineral engineering received starting offers averaging $64,404 a year.

Engineers who work for the federal government in its mining operations tend to earn less than their counterparts in the private oil and gas industries.

Depending on their employers, most mining engineers enjoy a full complement of benefits, including vacation and sick time as well as holidays and medical and dental insurance.

## WORK ENVIRONMENT

Engineers in the mining industry generally work where the mineral deposits are situated, often near small, rural communities. But those who specialize in research, management, consulting, or sales may work in metropolitan areas.

For those who work at the mine sites, conditions vary depending on the mine's location and structure and on what the engineer does. Conditions in the underground environment differ from those in surface mining. Natural light and fresh air are absent; temperatures may be uncomfortably hot or cold. Some mines have large amounts of water seeping into the openings. Potential hazards include caving ground, rockfalls, explosions from accumulation of gas or misuse of explosives, and poisonous gases. Most mines, however, are relatively safe and comfortable, owing to artificial light and ventilation, protective clothing, and water-pumping and ground-support systems.

Many mining engineers work a standard 40-hour week. In order to meet project deadlines, however, they may have to work longer hours under considerable stress.

## OUTLOOK

The demand for mining engineers is expected to grow faster than the average for all careers through 2018, according to the DOL. Opportunities for mining engineers should be good for several reasons. Demand is increasing for coal, metals, minerals, as well as the demand for products made from stone, clay, and glass. Additionally, many mining engineers are nearing retirement age. Since few students major in mining engineering, and only a few schools offer mining engineering programs, these vacant positions may not be completely filled by new graduates. Finally, U.S. mining engineers are increasingly sought after to work on projects in foreign countries. Mining engineers who are willing to work in foreign countries will have strong employment prospects.

Shortages in our natural resources will also create new opportunities for mining engineers. As mineral deposits are depleted, engineers will have to devise ways of mining less accessible low-grade ores to meet the demand for new alloys and new uses for minerals and metals. As more attention is placed on the environmental effects of mining, more engineers will be needed to provide expertise regarding land reclamation and water and air pollution.

## FOR MORE INFORMATION

*For information on careers, schools, college student membership, scholarships and grants, and other resources, contact*
The Minerals, Metals, and Materials Society
184 Thorn Hill Road
Warrendale, PA 15086-7514
Tel: 800-759-4867
http://www.tms.org

*For statistics on the mining industry, contact*
National Mining Association
101 Constitution Avenue, NW, Suite 500 East
Washington, DC 20001-2133
Tel: 202-463-2600
http://www.nma.org

*For information on educational programs, contact*
Society for Mining, Metallurgy, and Exploration
12999 East Adam Aircraft Circle
Englewood, CO 80112-4167
Tel: 800-763-3132
http://www.smenet.org

*For information on career opportunities, scholarships, and mentor*
*programs, contact*
Society of Women Engineers
120 South LaSalle Street, Suite 1515
Chicago, IL 60603-3572
Tel: 877-793-4636
E-mail: hq@swe.org
http://societyofwomenengineers.swe.org

## ━━━━━━━ INTERVIEW ━━━━━━━

*Dr. Rajive Ganguli, PE, is a professor of mining engineering and*
*the chairman of the Department of Mining and Geological Engi-*
*neering at the University of Alaska Fairbanks (UAF). He discussed*
*his career and the field of mining engineering with the editors of*
Careers in Focus: Energy.

**Q. Can you please tell us about your program and your
background?**

**A.** The Department of Mining and Geological Engineering at the
University of Alaska Fairbanks offers two bachelor of science
programs (Mining Engineering, Geological Engineering), three
master of science programs (Mining Engineering, Geological
Engineering, and Mineral Preparation Engineering), and a Ph.D.
in Engineering in two areas of concentration: Mining Engineering and Geological Engineering. The two undergraduate
programs are accredited by ABET, the national accreditation
agency of engineering programs. The students have access to
and operate our own underground mine, the Silver Fox Mine,
located 20 miles outside of Fairbanks.

The Mining Engineering program is one of the oldest in
the country, being one of the founding majors (1917) of UAF.
Graduates of our programs are at most of the major mines in
Alaska, and include Tom Albanese, currently the CEO of one
of the world's largest mining companies, Rio Tinto (based in
London).

As far as my background goes, I have three degrees in mining engineering: a bachelor of engineering (1991) from Osmania University, India; a master of science (1995) from Virginia Polytechnic and State University; and a Ph.D. (1999) from the University of Kentucky. I have worked in a surface copper mine (India) and an underground coal mine (Alabama). I am a registered professional engineer (mining) in Alaska, and an underground mine foreman (Alabama).

**Q. What type of internships are offered to students?**

**A.** Our students participate in paid engineering internships at mines, exploration companies, consulting companies, and government agencies nationwide. Employers include Usibelli Coal Mine, Fort Knox mine, Pogo mine (all Alaska), BHP Billiton (New Mexico), Barrick Gold (Nevada), Gold Canyon Mining (Nevada), and various agencies of the State of Alaska (Department of Transportation, Geological and Geophysical Survey, etc.). Many students obtain and do two to four paid summer engineering internships before graduating.

**Q. What is one thing that young people may not know about a career in mining engineering?**

**A.** A career in mining engineering gives them the ability to impact the future of the society. Mankind has an enormous appetite for material that cannot be grown. It interacts with the environment partly through the mining industry. A mining engineer, therefore, not only helps mankind live in a way they want to, but also controls the way it impacts the environment. If a young person truly wants to impact how we handle the environment, they should be in the mining industry.

**Q. What advice would you offer mining engineering majors as they graduate and look for jobs?**

**A.** Employers look for two things in a technically competent person: the ability to work with others and the ability to communicate. Therefore, fine-tune your people skills and improve your written and oral communication skills. To some extent, technical skills are second to these two abilities. Unfortunately, most engineering students are bad communicators as they think writing is for English majors.

**Q. What is the employment outlook for mining engineers? How is the field changing?**

**A.** The industry will see massive retirements in the next 10 years. Therefore, there will be many opportunities for fast growth for entry-level engineers.

Technically speaking, the biggest change is the level of automation and "data-driven" nature of mining. [There is] more real-time control, automation, etc. On the nontechnical side, the industry is realizing that public opinion matters. Massive projects can get delayed years due to bad press. This is certainly true in the Western world. Therefore, companies will take worker safety and social and environmental impacts more seriously in the future.

**Q. What has been one (or more) of your most rewarding experiences as a mining engineer and/or educator, and why?**

**A.** For me it has been the combination of industry experience and academia. I got to see the sense of "brotherhood" among miners when I was a foreman/engineer in India and in Alabama. I got to see the excitement, rewards, and challenges of life as miner. In academia, I get to influence budding engineers and impart my philosophy. As I write this e-mail, the miners are getting rescued in Chile. I was able to discuss it in class with the "future CEOs" and discussed with them what should have been done to prevent the incident in the first place.

# Nuclear Engineers

## OVERVIEW

*Nuclear engineers* are concerned with accessing, using, and controlling the energy released when the nucleus of an atom is split. The process of splitting atoms, called fission, produces a nuclear reaction, which creates radiation in addition to nuclear energy. Nuclear energy and radiation have many uses. Some engineers design, develop, and operate nuclear power plants, which are used to generate electricity and power navy ships. Others specialize in developing nuclear weapons, medical uses for radioactive materials, and disposal facilities for radioactive waste. There are approximately 16,900 nuclear engineers employed in the United States.

## HISTORY

Nuclear engineering as a formal science is quite young. However, part of its theoretical foundation rests with the ancient Greeks. In the 5th century B.C., Greek philosophers postulated that the building blocks of all matter were indestructible elements, which they named atomos, meaning "indivisible." This atomic theory was accepted for centuries, until the British chemist and physicist John Dalton revised it in the early 1800s. In the following century, scientific and mathematical experimentation led to the formation of modern atomic and nuclear theory.

Today, it is known that the atom is far from indivisible and that its dense center, the nucleus, can be split to create tremendous energy. The first occurrence of this splitting process was inadvertently induced in 1938 by two German chemists, Otto Hahn and Fritz Strassman. Further studies confirmed this process and established that the frag-

## QUICK FACTS

**School Subjects**
Mathematics
Physics

**Personal Skills**
Communication/ideas
Technical/scientific

**Work Environment**
Primarily indoors
Primarily one location

**Minimum Education Level**
Bachelor's degree

**Salary Range**
$66,590 to $96,910 to $140,140+

**Certification or Licensing**
Required for certain positions

**Outlook**
About as fast as the average

**DOT**
015

**GOE**
02.07.01

**NOC**
2132

**O*NET-SOC**
17-2161.00

ments resulting from the fission in turn strike the nuclei of other atoms, resulting in a chain reaction that produces constant energy.

The discipline of modern nuclear engineering is traced to 1942, when physicist Enrico Fermi and his colleagues produced the first self-sustained nuclear chain reaction in the first nuclear reactor ever built. In 1950, North Carolina State College offered the first accredited nuclear engineering program. By 1965, nuclear engineering programs had become widely available at universities and colleges throughout the country and worldwide. These programs provided engineers with a background in reactor physics and control, heat transfer, radiation effects, and shielding.

Current applications in the discipline of nuclear engineering include the use of reactors to propel naval vessels and the production of radioisotopes for medical purposes. Most of the growth in the nuclear industry, however, has focused on the production of electric energy.

Despite the controversy over the risks involved with atomic power, it continues to be used around the world for a variety of purposes. The Nuclear Energy Institute reports that 29 countries currently operate nuclear energy plants to produce electricity. In the United States, approximately 20 percent of the country's electricity is supplied by nuclear plants. In 2009, Vermont received 72.3 percent of its electricity from nuclear power, the highest of all states. Medicine,

## Leading States for Nuclear-Power-Generated Electricity

The following states had the largest percentage of their electricity generated by nuclear energy in 2009:

1. Vermont: 72.3 percent
2. New Jersey: 55.1 percent
3. Connecticut: 53.4 percent
4. South Carolina: 52.0 percent
5. Illinois: 48.7 percent
6. New Hampshire: 44.1 percent
7. Virginia: 39.6 percent

Source: Nuclear Energy Institute

manufacturing, and agriculture have also benefited from nuclear research. Such use requires the continued development of nuclear waste management. Low-level wastes, which result from power plants as well as hospitals and research facilities, must be reduced in volume, packed in leak-proof containers, and buried, and waste sites must be continually monitored.

## THE JOB

Nuclear engineers are involved in various aspects of the generation, use, and maintenance of nuclear energy and the safe disposal of its waste. Nuclear engineers work on research and development, design, fuel management, safety analysis, operation and testing, sales, and education. Their contributions affect consumer and industrial power supplies, medical technology, the food industry, and other industries.

Nuclear engineering is dominated by the power industry. Some engineers work for companies that manufacture reactors. They research, develop, design, manufacture, and install parts used in these facilities, such as core supports, reflectors, thermal shields, biological shields, instrumentation, and safety and control systems.

Those who are responsible for the maintenance of power plants must monitor operations efficiently and guarantee that facilities meet safety standards. Nuclear energy activities in the United States are closely supervised and regulated by government and independent agencies, especially the Nuclear Regulatory Commission (NRC). The NRC oversees the use of nuclear materials by electric utility companies throughout the United States. NRC employees ensure the safety of nongovernment nuclear materials and facilities and make sure that related operations do not adversely affect public health or the environment. Nuclear engineers who work for regulatory agencies establish the standards that all organizations involved with nuclear energy must follow. They issue licenses, establish rules, implement safety research, perform risk analyses, conduct on-site inspections, and pursue research. The NRC is one of the main regulatory agencies employing nuclear engineers.

Many nuclear engineers work directly with public electric utility companies. Tasks are diverse, and teams of engineers are responsible for supervising construction and operation, analyzing safety, managing fuel, assessing environmental impact, training personnel, managing the plant, storing spent fuel, managing waste, and analyzing economic factors.

Some engineers working for nuclear power plants focus on the quality of the water supply. Their plants extract salt from water, and engineers develop new methods and designs for such desalinization systems.

The food supply also benefits from the work of nuclear engineers. Nuclear energy is used for pasteurization and sterilization, insect and pest control, and fertilizer production. Furthermore, nuclear engineers conduct genetic research on improving various food strains and their resistance to harmful elements.

Nuclear engineers in the medical field design and construct equipment for diagnosing and treating illnesses and disease. They perform research on radioisotopes, which are produced by nuclear reactions. Radioisotopes are used in heart pacemakers, in X-ray equipment, and for sterilizing medical instruments. According to the Nuclear Energy Institute, approximately 4,000 nuclear medicine departments at hospitals across the country perform, on an annual basis, more than 18 million patient procedures.

Nuclear engineers perform numerous other jobs. *Nuclear health physicists, nuclear criticality safety engineers,* and *radiation protection technicians* conduct research and training programs designed to protect plant and laboratory employees against radiation hazards. *Nuclear fuels research engineers* and *nuclear fuels reclamation engineers* work with reprocessing systems for atomic fuels. *Accelerator operators* coordinate the operation of equipment used in experiments on subatomic particles, and *scanners* work with photographs, produced by particle detectors, of atomic collisions.

## REQUIREMENTS

### High School

If you are interested in becoming a professional engineer, you must begin preparing yourself in high school. You should take honors-level courses in mathematics and the sciences. Specifically, you should complete courses in algebra, geometry, trigonometry, and calculus, chemistry, physics, and biology. Take English, social studies, and a foreign language (many published technical papers that are required reading in later years are written in German or French). Be sure to keep your computer skills up to date by taking computer science classes.

### Postsecondary Training

Professional engineers must have at least a bachelor's degree. You should attend a four-year college or university that is approved by the Accreditation Board for Engineering and Technology (http://www.abet.org). In a nuclear engineering program, you will focus on subjects similar to those studied in high school but at a more advanced level. Courses also include engineering sciences and atomic and nuclear physics.

These subjects will prepare you for analyzing and designing nuclear systems and understanding how they operate. You will learn and comprehend what is involved in the interaction between radiation and matter; radiation measurements; the production and use of radioisotopes; reactor physics and engineering; and fusion reactions. The subject of safety will be emphasized, particularly with regard to handling radiation sources and implementing nuclear systems.

You must have a master's or doctoral degree for most jobs in research and higher education, and for supervisory and administrative positions. It is recommended that you obtain a graduate degree in nuclear engineering because this level of education will help you obtain the skills required for advanced specialization in the field. Many institutions that offer advanced degrees have nuclear reactors and well-equipped laboratories for teaching and research. You can obtain information about these schools by contacting the U.S. Department of Energy (http://www.energy.gov).

### Certification or Licensing

A professional engineer (PE) license is usually required before obtaining employment on public projects (i.e., work that may affect life, health, or property). Although registration guidelines differ for each state, most states require a degree from an accredited engineering program, four years of work experience in the field, and a minimum grade on a state exam. For more information on licensing and examination requirements, visit the National Council of Examiners for Engineering and Surveying's Web site, http://www.ncees.org.

### Other Requirements

Nuclear engineers will encounter two unique concerns. First, exposure to high levels of radiation may be hazardous; thus, engineers must always follow safety measures. Those working near radioactive materials must adhere to strict precautions outlined by regulatory standards. In addition, female engineers of childbearing age may not be allowed to work in certain areas or perform certain duties because of the potential harm to the human fetus from radiation.

Finally, nuclear engineers must be prepared for a lifetime of continuing education. Because nuclear engineering is founded in the fundamental theories of physics and the notions of atomic and nuclear theory are difficult to conceptualize except mathematically, an aptitude for physics, mathematics, and chemistry is indispensable.

## EXPLORING

If you are interested in becoming an engineer, you can join science clubs such as the Junior Engineering Technical Society (JETS). Its e-newsletter *JETS News* (http://www.jets.org/newsletter) will introduce you to engineering careers and a wide variety of engineering-related resources. If you are a more advanced student, you may want to read materials published by the American Nuclear Society (http://www.ans.org). You may also want to join science clubs, which provide the opportunity to work with others, design engineering projects, and participate in career exploration.

## EMPLOYERS

Nuclear engineers work in a variety of settings. According to the U.S. Department of Labor (DOL), approximately 16,900 nuclear engineers are employed in the United States. Engineers work in the utilities field; for professional, scientific, and technical services firms; and for the federal government. Of those who work for the federal government, many are civilian employees of the navy, and most of the rest work for the U.S. Department of Energy. Some nuclear engineers work for defense manufacturers or manufacturers of nuclear power equipment.

## STARTING OUT

Most students begin their job search while still in college, collecting advice from job counselors and their schools' career services centers and using organizations and Web sites to find open positions. For example, the Society of Women Engineers (SWE) offers members the opportunity to post their resumes or find job matches through its Web site. Networking with those already employed in the field is an excellent way to find out about job openings. Networking opportunities are available during meetings of professional organizations, such as the SWE annual national conference.

## ADVANCEMENT

Because the nuclear engineering field is so young, the time is ripe for technological developments, and engineers must therefore keep abreast of new research and technology throughout their careers. Advancement for engineers is contingent upon continuing education, research activity, and on-the-job expertise.

As with other engineering disciplines, a hierarchy of workers exists, with the *chief engineer* having overall authority over managers and project engineers. This is true whether you are working in research, design, production, sales, or teaching. After gaining a certain amount of experience, engineers may apply for positions in supervision and management.

Advancement may also bring recognition in the form of grants, scholarships, fellowships, and awards. For example, the American Nuclear Society has established the Landis Young Member Engineering Achievement Award to recognize outstanding work performed by members. To be eligible for this award, you must be younger than 40 years old and demonstrate effective application of engineering knowledge that results in a concept, design, analysis method, or product used in nuclear power research and development or in a manufacturing application.

## EARNINGS

Nuclear engineers earned a median income of $96,910 in 2009, according to the DOL. The department also reports that the highest paid 10 percent of nuclear engineers earned more than $140,140, while the lowest paid 10 percent earned less than $66,590 annually. Nuclear engineers working for the federal government earned an average of $94,740 in 2009.

Benefits offered depend on the employer but generally include paid vacation and sick days, health insurance, and retirement plans.

## WORK ENVIRONMENT

In general, nuclear engineering is a technically demanding and politically volatile field. Those who work daily at power plants perhaps incur the most stress because they are responsible for preventing large-scale accidents involving radiation. Those who work directly with nuclear energy face risks associated with radiation contamination. Engineers handling the disposal of hazardous material also work under stressful conditions because they must take tremendous care to ensure the public's health and safety.

Research, teaching, and design occupations allow engineers to work in laboratories, classrooms, and industrial manufacturing facilities. Many engineers who are not directly involved with the physical maintenance of nuclear facilities spend most of their working hours, an average of 46 hours per week, conducting research.

Most work at desks and must have the ability to concentrate on very detailed data for long periods of time, drawing up plans and constructing models of nuclear applications.

## OUTLOOK

Employment for nuclear engineers is expected to grow about as fast as the average for all careers through 2018, according to the DOL. Only a small number of people graduate from nuclear engineering programs each year, which will create good job prospects.

With the support of the federal government, the nuclear industry hopes to build new plants. The recent energy crisis in California and the public's growing acceptance of nuclear power is helping to fuel the need for more plants, and will create improved employment opportunities for nuclear engineers in the near future. In addition to working in plants, nuclear engineers will also be needed to work in defense-related areas, to develop nuclear-related medical technology, and to monitor and improve waste management and safety standards.

## FOR MORE INFORMATION

*For information on scholarships, education, and careers, contact*
**American Nuclear Society**
555 North Kensington Avenue
LaGrange Park, IL 60526-5535
Tel: 708-352-6611
http://www.ans.org

*For information on student membership, contact*
**Junior Engineering Technical Society**
1420 King Street, Suite 405
Alexandria, VA 22314-2750
Tel: 703-548-5387
E-mail: info@jets.org
http://www.jets.org

*For a wide variety of career and industry information, contact*
**Nuclear Energy Institute**
1776 I Street, NW, Suite 400
Washington, DC 20006-3708
Tel: 202-739-8000
http://www.nei.org

*For career guidance and scholarship information, contact*
**Society of Women Engineers**
120 South LaSalle Street, Suite 1515
Chicago, IL 60603-3572
Tel: 877-793-4636
E-mail: hq@swe.org
http://societyofwomenengineers.swe.org

*For information on careers and nuclear power, contact*
**U.S. Department of Energy**
1000 Independence Avenue, SW
Washington, DC 20585-0001
Tel: 202-586-5000
http://www.energy.gov

*For information on careers and training, visit*
**Get Into Energy**
http://www.getintoenergy.com

# Nuclear Reactor Operators and Technicians

## OVERVIEW

Licensed *nuclear reactor operators* work in nuclear power plant control rooms where they monitor instruments that record the performance of every pump, compressor, and other treatment system in the reactor unit. Nuclear power plants must have operators on duty at all times. In addition to monitoring the instruments in the control room, the nuclear reactor operator runs periodic tests on equipment at the station. *Nuclear reactor operator technicians* are in training to become operators; they study nuclear science theory and learn to perform reactor operation and control activities. They work under the supervision of licensed nuclear reactor operators, and later they work as beginning operators. *Senior operators,* or *senior reactor operators,* have further training and experience and oversee the activities of nuclear reactor operators and technicians. Approximately 5,000 nuclear reactor operators and 6,400 nuclear technicians are employed in the United States.

## HISTORY

The potential for nuclear power generation was first demonstrated in 1942, when a group of scientists led by Enrico Fermi conducted the first controlled nuclear chain reaction in a nuclear reactor located under the football stands on Stagg Field at the University of Chicago. After World War II, research continued on peacetime uses of controlled atomic energy. In 1948, researchers increasingly emphasized the design of nuclear power reactors to generate electricity.

By late 1963, the technology for these nuclear reactors was ready for commercial use, and the first nuclear power plants were constructed. Their successful operation and the low cost of the electric power they generated were promising. Further development of technology continued, and the construction of several additional nuclear power plants began.

Since then, the field has learned a great deal about the design and safe operation of nuclear-fueled electric power plants. Quality assurance and control procedures have been developed to ensure that every step of a plant's construction and operation meets the necessary safety requirements.

Specific procedures are in place to protect against radiation, and special technicians work in each plant to ensure the least possible risk of radiation exposure to workers. Studies show that the safest operation of nuclear plants is directly attributable to carefully selected and thoroughly trained nuclear reactor operators. Since 1963, tens of thousands of people have been trained and licensed by the federal government to work as nuclear reactor operators.

## THE JOB

The nuclear reactor is like an engine providing power, in the form of hot steam, to run the entire nuclear power plant. Nuclear reactor operators are the nuclear station's driver, in the sense that they control all the machines used to generate power at the station. Working under the direction of a *plant manager,* the nuclear reactor operator is responsible for the continuous and safe operation of a reactor. Although most nuclear power plants contain more than one nuclear reactor unit, each nuclear reactor operator is responsible for only one of the units.

From the standpoint of safety and uninterrupted operation, the nuclear reactor operator holds the most critical job in the plant. The operator's performance is considered so essential that any shutdown of an average 1,000-megawatt plant, whether due to an accident or operating error, can result in a minimum loss of the cost of the operator's salary for 10 years.

Licensed nuclear reactor operators work in the station control room, monitoring meters and gauges. They read and interpret instruments that record the performance of every valve, pump,

## Top 10 Nuclear-Generating Countries

The following countries generated the largest amount of nuclear energy in 2009:

| Country | Billion kWh |
| --- | --- |
| 1. United States | 798.7 |
| 2. France | 390.0 |
| 3. Japan | 260.1 |
| 4. Russia | 153.0 |
| 5. Republic of Korea | 141.1 |
| 6. Germany | 127.6 |
| 7. Canada | 85.3 |
| 8. Ukraine | 77.8 |
| 9. China | 70.1 |
| 10. United Kingdom | 62.9 |

Sources: Energy Information Administration, International Atomic Energy Agency

compressor, switch, and water treatment system in the reactor unit. When necessary, they make adjustments to fission rate, pressure, water temperature, and the flow rate of the various pieces of equipment to ensure safe and efficient operation.

During each 24-hour period, operators make rounds four times. This task involves reviewing the unit's control board and recording the readings of the instruments. Each hour, a computer generates a reading indicating the amount of power the unit is generating.

In addition to monitoring the instruments in the control room, the nuclear reactor operator runs periodic tests, including pressure readings, flow readings, and vibration analyses on each piece of equipment. The operator must also perform logic testing on the electrical components in order to check the built-in safeguards.

Every 12 to 18 months, the nuclear reactor operator must also refuel the reactor unit, a procedure that is sometimes called an outage. During the refueling, the turbine is brought offline, or shut down. After it cools and depressurizes, the unit is opened, and any repairs, testing, and preventive maintenance are taken care of. Depleted nuclear fuel is exchanged for new fuel. The unit is then repressurized, reheated, and brought back online, or restarted.

*Auxiliary equipment operators* normally work at the site of the equipment. Their work can include anything from turning a valve to bringing a piece of equipment in and out of service. All of their requests for action on any of the machines must be approved by the nuclear reactor operator.

Precise operation is required in nuclear power plants to be sure that radiation does not contaminate the equipment, the operating personnel, or the nearby population and environment. The most serious danger is the release of large amounts of atomic radiation into the atmosphere. Operating personnel are directly involved in the prevention of reactor accidents and in the containment of radioactivity in the event of an accident.

Nuclear reactor operators always begin their employment as technicians. In this capacity, they gain plant experience and technical knowledge at a functioning nuclear power plant. The technician trains on a simulator and studies the reactor and control room. A simulator is built and equipped as an operating reactor control station. Technicians can practice operating the reactor and learn what readings the instruments in the simulator give when certain adjustments are made in the reactor control settings. This company-sponsored training is provided to help technicians attain the expertise necessary to obtain an operator's license. Even after obtaining a license, however, beginning operators work under the direction of a shift supervisor, senior operator, or other management personnel.

# REQUIREMENTS

Although a college degree is not required, many utilities prefer candidates to have some postsecondary training. More and more nuclear reactor operators have completed at least two years of college, and about 25 percent have a four-year degree. Lack of college experience, however, does not exclude an applicant from being hired. High school graduates are selected based on subjects studied and aptitude test results.

## High School

If you wish to enter nuclear technology programs, you should study algebra, geometry, English composition, blueprint reading, and chemistry and physics with laboratory study. In addition, classes in computer science and beginning electronics will help you prepare for the technology program that follows high school.

## Postsecondary Training

In the first year of a nuclear technology program at a technical or community college, you will probably take nuclear technology, radiation physics, applied mathematics, electricity and electronics, technical communications, basic industrial economics, radiation detection and measurement, inorganic chemistry, radiation protection, mathematics, basic mechanics, quality assurance and quality control, principles of process instrumentation, heat transfer and fluid flow, metallurgy, and metal properties.

In the second year, you may be required to take technical writing and reporting, nuclear systems, blueprint reading, mechanical component characteristics and specifications, reactor physics, reactor safety, power plant systems, instrumentation and control of reactors and plant systems, power plant chemistry, reactor operations, reactor auxiliary systems, and industrial organizations and institutions.

Upon completing a technical program, you will continue training once you are employed at a plant. On-the-job training includes learning nuclear science theory; radiation detection; and reactor design, operation, and control. In addition, nuclear reactor operator technicians must learn in detail how the nuclear power plant works. Trainees are assigned to a series of work–learn tasks that take them to all parts of the plant. If trainees have been working in the plant as regular employees, their individual training is planned around what they already know. This kind of training usually takes two to three years and includes simulator practice.

The simulator is an exact replica of the station's real control room. The controls in the simulator are connected to an interactive software program. Working under the supervision of a licensed nuclear reactor operator, trainees experience mock events in the simulator, which teach them how to safely handle emergencies.

During this on-the-job training, technicians learn about nuclear power plant materials, processes, material balances, plant operating equipment, pipe systems, electrical systems, and process control. It is crucial to understand how each activity within the unit affects other instruments or systems. Nuclear reactor operator technicians are given written and oral exams, sometimes as often as once a week. In some companies, technicians are dismissed from their job for failing to pass any one training exam.

Some people in the industry believe that one of the most difficult aspects of becoming a nuclear reactor operator is getting hired. Because electric utilities invest a substantial amount of time and money to train nuclear reactor operators, they are extremely selective when hiring.

The application process entails intensive screening, including identity checks, FBI fingerprint checks, drug and alcohol tests, psychological tests, and credit checks. After passing this initial screening, the applicant takes a range of mathematical and science aptitude tests.

Utility companies recruit most nuclear reactor operator technicians from local high schools and colleges, fossil fuel plants (utilities using nonnuclear sources of energy), and U.S. Navy nuclear programs. Knowledge of nuclear science and the discipline and professionalism gained from navy experience make veterans excellent candidates. Graduates of two-year programs in nuclear technology also make excellent trainees because they are well versed in nuclear and power plant fundamentals.

The standards and course content for all nuclear training programs are established by the Nuclear Regulatory Commission (NRC). In addition, each nuclear power plant training program must be accredited by the Institute of Nuclear Power Operations, which was founded in 1979 by industry leaders to promote excellence in nuclear plant operations.

## Certification or Licensing

Nuclear reactor operators are required to be licensed, based on examinations given by the NRC. The licensing process involves passing several exams, including a physical exam. The first written exam (Generic Fundamentals Examination) covers topics such as reactor theory and thermodynamics. Candidates who pass this exam then take a site-specific exam that includes a written section and an operating test on the power plant's simulator. Candidates who pass these tests receive their licenses. A license is valid for six years and only for the specific power plant for which the candidate applied.

To maintain their licenses, operators must pass an annual practical, or operating, exam and a written requalification exam given by their employers. Requirements for license renewal include certification from the employer that the operator has successfully completed requalification and operating exams and passed a physical.

## Other Requirements

Nuclear reactor operators are subject to continuous exams and ongoing training. They must be diligent about keeping their skills and knowledge up-to-date. A desire for lifelong learning, therefore, is necessary for those doing this work.

Because of the dangerous nature of nuclear energy, the nuclear reactor operator's performance is critical to the safety of other employees, the community, and the environment. Operators must perform their job with a high degree of precision and accuracy. They must be able to remain calm under pressure and maintain sound judgment in emergencies.

Although nuclear reactor operators must frequently perform numerous tasks at once, they must also be able to remain alert during quiet times and handle the monotony of routine readings and tests.

Responding to requests from other personnel, such as the auxiliary operators, is a regular part of the nuclear reactor operator's job. The ability to communicate and work well with other team members and plant personnel is essential.

## EXPLORING

High school counselors and advisers at community or technical colleges are good sources of information about a career as a nuclear reactor operator. The librarians in these institutions also may be helpful in directing you to introductory publications and Web sites on nuclear reactors.

Opportunities for exploring a career as a nuclear reactor operator are limited because nuclear power plants are usually located in places relatively far from schools and have strictly limited visiting policies. Very few commercial or research reactors provide tours for the general public. However, many utility companies with nuclear power plants have visitors' centers, where tours are scheduled at specified hours. In addition, interested high school students usually can arrange visits to nonnuclear power plants, which allows them to learn about the energy-conversion process common to all steam-powered electric power generation plants.

## EMPLOYERS

There are 104 commercial nuclear power plants operating in 31 states in the United States, according to the Nuclear Energy Institute. In addition, there are approximately 36 reactors used for research and training at educational and other institutions, according to the NRC. Nuclear reactor operators, naturally, work at nuclear power plants and are employed by utility or energy companies, universities, and other institutions operating these facilities.

## STARTING OUT

In recent years, nuclear technology programs have been the best source for hiring nuclear reactor operator technicians. Students are usually interviewed and hired by the nuclear power plant personnel recruiters toward the end of their technical college program and start working in the power plant as trainees after they graduate.

Navy veterans from nuclear programs and employees from other parts of the nuclear power plant may also be good candidates for entering a nuclear reactor operator training program.

## ADVANCEMENT

Many licensed reactor operators progress to the position of senior reactor operator (as they gain experience and undergo further study). To be certified as senior reactor operators (SROs), operators must pass the senior reactor operator exam, which requires a broader and more detailed knowledge of the power plant, plant procedures, and company policies. In some locations, the senior reactor operator may supervise other licensed operators.

SROs may also advance into the positions of field foreman and then control room supervisor or unit supervisor. These are management positions, and supervisors are responsible for an operating crew. Successful supervisors can be promoted to shift engineer or even plant manager.

Licensed nuclear reactor operators and senior reactor operators may also become part of a power plant's education staff or gain employment in a technical or four-year college, company employee training department, or an outside consulting company. Both operators and SROs may work for reactor manufacturers and serve as research and development consultants. They also may teach trainees to use simulators or operating models of the manufacturer's reactors. Finally, operators and SROs may work for the NRC, which administers licensing examinations.

## EARNINGS

Nuclear reactor operators earned an annual median income of $72,650 in 2009, according to the U.S. Department of Labor (DOL). Salaries ranged from less than $54,590 to more than $100,310 a year.

The starting salary rate for nuclear reactor operator technicians depends on the technician's knowledge of nuclear science theory and work experience. Graduates of strong nuclear technology programs or former navy nuclear technicians usually earn more than people without this background or training. Salaries also vary among different electric power companies.

The DOL reports that nuclear technicians (including those assisting in production) earned a median salary of $67,340 in 2009, with salaries ranging from less than $41,330 to $92,580 or more a year.

In addition to a base salary, some workers are paid a premium for working certain shifts and overtime. Standard benefits include insurance, paid holidays, vacations, and retirement benefits.

Employers also pay for the continued formal and on-the-job training of nuclear reactor operators. Of licensed reactor operator staff members, 10 to 20 percent are in formal retraining programs at any one time to renew their operator's licenses or to obtain a senior operator's license.

## WORK ENVIRONMENT

Nuclear reactor operator technicians spend their working hours in classrooms and laboratories, learning about every part of the power plant. Toward the end of their training, they work at a reactor control-room simulator or in the control room of an operational reactor unit under the direction of licensed operators.

Operators work in clean and well-lit, but windowless, control rooms. Because nuclear reactor operators spend most of their time in the control room, employers have made great efforts to make it as comfortable as possible. Some control rooms are painted in bright, stimulating colors and some are kept a little cooler than is standard in most offices. Some utilities have even supplied exercise equipment for their nuclear reactor operators to use during quiet times.

Because nuclear reactors must operate continuously, operators usually work an eight-hour shift and rotate through each of three shifts, taking turns as required. This means operators will work weekends as well as nights some of the time. During their shift, most operators are required to remain in the control room, often eating their lunches at their station. Being in the same environment for eight hours at a time with the same crew members can be stressful.

Although nuclear reactor operators may work at one station of control boards for a long time, they are not allowed to personalize their space because each station is used by more than one person as the shifts rotate.

Although most operators do not wear suits to work, they dress in office attire. Technicians, however, will spend part of their training outside the reactor area. In this environment, appropriate clothing is worn, including hard hats and safety shoes, if necessary.

Operators are shielded from radiation by the concrete outside wall of the reactor containment vessel. If leaks should occur, operators are less subject to exposure than plant personnel who are more directly involved in maintenance and inspection. Nonetheless, technicians wear film badges that darken with radiation exposure. In addition, radiation measurement is carried out in all areas of the plant and plant surroundings according to a regular schedule.

The tough scrutiny of the NRC is an added stress for operators. Plant management, the local community, and the national and local press also watch for compliance with regulatory and safety measures.

A career as a nuclear reactor operator offers the opportunity to assume a high degree of responsibility and to be paid while training. People who enjoy using precision instruments and learning about the latest technological developments are likely to find this career appealing. Operators must be able to shoulder a high degree of responsibility and to work well under stressful conditions. They must be emotionally stable and calm at all times, even in emergencies.

## OUTLOOK

Employment for nuclear power plant operators is expected to experience little or no change through 2018, while employment for technicians is expected to grow about as fast as the average for all occupations, according to the DOL. Newly enacted NRC regulations that seek to reduce worker fatigue by limiting the length of worker shifts will create demand for workers. Also, new nuclear plants are expected to be built during the next decade, which will create demand for operators and technicians.

Questions regarding the safety of nuclear power, the environmental effects of nuclear plants, and the safe disposal of radioactive waste have been of public concern since the occurrence of major accidents at the Three Mile Island (United States, 1979) and Chernobyl (Ukraine, 1986) plants, as well as the more recent meltdown at the Fukushima Daiichi ("Number One") plant in Japan in 2011. The Japanese plant was damaged as a result of a devastating earthquake and tsunami. In the immediate aftermath of the accident, 58 percent of Americans surveyed by ORC International for the nonpartisan Civil Society Institute said that they would be less supportive of an expansion of nuclear power. It is too early to tell what the long-term effects of the emergency at the Fukushima Daiichi plant will be on the use of nuclear power. As time passes, Americans may be more amenable to the use of nuclear energy—especially as U.S. fossil fuel resources continue to diminish and energy prices continue to increase. Given these developments, it is estimated that the construction of nuclear plants will eventually resume—although there will be an increasing emphasis on safety.

Many unresolved questions remain about environmental effects and waste disposal and reprocessing. In addition, construction and maintenance costs of nuclear power plants have increased rapidly due to changes in the requirements for power plant design and safety. Until these issues are resolved, the future of the nuclear industry will remain uncertain.

## FOR MORE INFORMATION

*For information on publications, scholarships, and seminars, contact*
American Nuclear Society
555 North Kensington Avenue
LaGrange Park, IL 60526-5535
Tel: 708-352-6611
http://www.new.ans.org

*This organization advocates the peaceful use of nuclear technologies. Visit its Web site for more information.*
American Society for Nondestructive Testing
PO Box 28518
1711 Arlingate Lane
Columbus, OH 43228-0518
Tel: 800-222-2768
http://www.asnt.org

*For information on the nuclear industry and careers, as well as a list of academic programs in nuclear energy, contact*
Nuclear Energy Institute
1776 I Street, NW, Suite 400
Washington, DC 20006-3708
Tel: 202-739-8000
http://www.nei.org

*For information on licensing, contact*
U.S. Nuclear Regulatory Commission
Washington, DC 20555-0001
Tel: 800-368-5642
http://www.nrc.gov

# Occupational Safety and Health Workers

## OVERVIEW

Occupational safety and health workers are responsible for the prevention of work-related accidents and diseases, injuries from unsafe products and practices, property losses from accidents and fires, and adverse effects of industrial processes on the environment. There are approximately 55,800 occupational safety specialists and 10,900 technicians employed in the United States.

## HISTORY

For thousands of years, people thought that accidents and illnesses just happened, or they blamed such unfortunate occurrences on fate, the wrath of the gods, or evil forces. Very little was done to prevent accidents systematically other than to wear charms, offer sacrifices, or engage in other rituals or behaviors thought to be preventive. At the same time, the slave trade reinforced the concept that certain workers' lives were expendable. The builders of the great ancient structures gave no thought to the well-being of their human inventory other than giving them enough food so that they were strong enough to work.

Throughout history many types of workers have been compelled to accept their lot in life. Even in more modern times, the early history of the industrial revolution demonstrated that workers were considered less important than the machines they operated or the output of a factory or mine. Little relationship was seen between productivity and the safety and health of the workers.

These exploitative practices were eventually halted through the joint efforts of social reform movements, labor unions, and progressive politicians. The rapid growth of technology in the 20th century made it possible to design machinery and equipment with built-in safety mechanisms. As medical research increased our knowledge of the effect of the working environment on health, psychological studies made us aware of the human factors that may lead to accident or illness. Labor unions and the federal government increased the pressure on companies to pay more attention to workplace conditions and the welfare of workers.

Now in the 21st century, we are probably safer at work than in most other places, including the home. Companies of all sizes have instituted practical safety measures and reduced worker hazards by developing new machinery and devising better safeguards. At the same time, they have established work safety rules and safety education programs for their workers. To protect the well-being and productivity of their workers, companies continue to allocate large sums to research and development in this area.

## THE JOB

Safety and health workers have a variety of responsibilities, which fall into four basic areas.

First, they identify and evaluate hazardous conditions and practices. They inspect facilities and equipment, conduct accident investigations, analyze work procedures, study building layouts, and consult with workers who are exposed to hazardous conditions.

Second, safety and health workers develop ways to control hazards. They observe, analyze, and solve problems using deductive reasoning and creativity.

### U.S. Energy Sources, 2009

Oil: 37 percent

Natural gas: 25 percent

Coal: 21 percent

Nuclear: 9 percent

Renewable: 8 percent

Source: Energy Information Administration

Third, safety personnel communicate hazard-control information to workers and management.

Fourth, safety personnel continually measure hazard-control systems and adjust them as needed. Safety employees gather information from accident investigations, inspections, customer or employee complaints, and other sources, such as government agencies and regulations. They may employ such strategies as designing or redesigning equipment and machinery, providing physical safeguards (for example, protective concrete shielding in nuclear reactors), or training workers in the use of safe procedures.

*Safety engineers* are primarily concerned with preventing accidents. In a large industrial plant, they may develop a safety program that covers several thousand employees. They examine plans for new machinery and equipment to see that all safety precautions have been included and put in place. They determine the weight-bearing capacity of the plant floor. They inspect existing machinery and design, build, and install safeguards where necessary. Many safety engineers work with *design engineers* to develop safe models of their company's products and monitor the manufacturing process to make sure the finished product is safe and reliable to use.

If an accident occurs, safety engineers investigate the cause. If the accident is related to a mechanical problem, they use their technical skills to correct it and prevent a recurrence. If it is because of human error, they may educate the particular workers in proper safety procedures and draw up an education program for the entire staff.

Safety engineers who work for trucking companies are known as *safety coordinators*. They work with both management and drivers to reduce losses due to accidents. They instruct truck-and-trailer drivers in matters pertaining to traffic and safety regulations and care of the equipment. They ride with drivers and patrol highways to detect errors in handling cargo and driving the vehicle. They also watch for any violations of company regulations and observe the conditions of the vehicles and the roads. They investigate accidents and recommend measures to improve safety records and lengthen the life of equipment.

*Occupational safety and health inspectors* work for government and regulatory agencies. They visit workplaces to detect unsafe machinery and equipment or to check for unhealthy working conditions. They discuss their findings with the employer or plant manager and request immediate correction of violations in accordance with federal, state, and local government standards and regulations.

In the mining industry, *mining inspectors* inspect underground and open-pit mines to ensure compliance with health and safety laws. They check timber supports, electrical and mechanical equipment, storage of explosives, and other possible hazards. They test the air for toxic or explosive gas or dust. They may also design safety devices and protective equipment for mine workers, lead rescue activities in the event of an emergency, and instruct mine workers in safety and first-aid procedures.

The light, heat, and power industry employs safety engineers (known as *safety inspectors*) to ensure the safety of the workers who construct and maintain overhead and underground power lines. Safety inspectors check safety belts, ladders, ropes, and tools; observe crews at work to make sure they use goggles, rubber gloves, and other safety devices; and examine the condition of tunnels and ditches. They investigate accidents, devise preventive measures, and instruct workers in safety matters.

*Fire protection engineers* have different tasks depending on where they work. In general, their job is to safeguard life and property against fire, explosion, and related hazards. Those employed by design and consulting firms work with architects and other engineers to build fire safety into new buildings. They study buildings before and after completion for such factors as fire resistance, the use and contents of the buildings, water supplies, and entrance and exit facilities. Fire protection engineers who work for manufacturers of fire equipment design alarm systems, fire-detection mechanisms, and fire-extinguishing devices and systems. They also investigate causes of accidental fires and may organize and train personnel to carry out fire-protection programs.

*Fire prevention research engineers* conduct research to determine the causes of fires and methods for preventing them. They study such problems as fires in high-rise buildings, and they test fire retardants and the fire safety of building materials. The results of such research are then used by fire protection engineers in the field. Fire prevention research engineers also prepare educational materials on fire prevention for insurance companies.

*Fire marshals* supervise and coordinate the activities of the fire-fighters in large industrial establishments such as refineries and auto plants. They also inspect equipment such as sprinklers and extinguishers; inspect the premises for combustion hazards and violations of fire ordinances; conduct fire drills; and direct fire-fighting and rescue activities in case of emergencies.

While safety and fire prevention engineers work to prevent accidents, *industrial hygienists* are concerned with the health of the

A state inspector checks a section of a mine that has been closed in order to determine if there are any explosive amounts of methane. *(Lee Smith, AP Photo)*

employees in the workplace. They collect and analyze samples of dust, gases, vapors, and other potentially toxic material; investigate the adequacy of ventilation, exhaust equipment, lighting, and other conditions that may affect employee health, comfort, or efficiency; evaluate workers' exposure to radiation and to noise; and recommend ways of controlling or eliminating such hazards. These hygienists work at the job site.

Other industrial hygienists work in the private laboratories of insurance, industrial, or consulting companies, where they analyze air samples, research health equipment, or investigate the effects of chemicals. *Health physicists* are specialists in radiation. Still other industrial hygienists specialize in the problems of air and water pollution.

*Environmental safety and health workers* prevent hazards to the environment and are concerned with pollution control, energy efficiency, recycling, waste disposal, and compliance with the government's Environmental Protection Agency requirements.

*Loss-control* and *occupational health consultants* are safety inspectors hired by property-liability insurance companies to perform services for their clients. They inspect insured properties and evaluate the physical conditions, safety practices, and hazardous situations that may exist; determine whether the client is an acceptable risk; calculate the amount of the insurance premium; and develop and monitor a program to eliminate or reduce all hazards. They also help set up health programs and medical services and train safety personnel.

## REQUIREMENTS

### High School

If you are interested in becoming an occupational safety and health worker, you will need to earn a bachelor's degree at the minimum. Therefore, while you are in high school, take a college preparatory course of study. Subjects that you should concentrate on include mathematics and sciences. Especially important are algebra, trigonometry, calculus, biology, chemistry, and physics. Because this work is so involved with people and their reactions to environments, you may also want to take psychology courses. Finally, because part of your work will include writing reports, giving presentations, and explaining changes to others, you will need to develop both your oral and written communication skills. To do this, take English and speech classes throughout your high school years.

### Postsecondary Training

For your postsecondary education, you should plan on getting a bachelor's degree in engineering or in one of the physical or biological sciences. Employers usually prefer to hire a candidate with a bachelor's or master's degree that is specifically related to occupational safety and health, such as safety engineering or management, industrial hygiene, fire-protection engineering, public health, or health physics. Degrees in chemical or mechanical engineering are also very desirable. According to the American Society of Safety Engineers (ASSE), more than 125 colleges and universities offer degrees in safety management, occupational safety, environmental protection, or a related field. In addition to the schools offering safety degrees, some engineering schools offer a safety specialty within their traditional engineering degree programs. Many schools with safety-degree programs are having difficulty accommodating the growing interest in an occupational safety education and have long waiting lists of students. These schools, however, have no trouble placing their graduates in jobs. The ASSE and some private foundations offer scholarships.

Employers are increasingly interested in hiring people who have knowledge of the three major categories in occupational safety and health: safety, industrial hygiene, and environmental management. Therefore, you should try to combine your studies; for example, if you major in safety, then you should minor in environmental affairs, or vice versa.

Workers in this field must keep abreast of new and changing trends and technologies. For this reason, many insurance companies provide training seminars and correspondence courses for the members of their staff. The Occupational Safety and Health Administration offers courses on topics such as occupational injury investigation and radiological health hazards. The ASSE, the National Safety Council, and other groups also provide continuing professional education for safety engineers.

In some cases you may be able to find employment with only a two-year degree, working as a safety and health technician. To advance in the field, however, you will need to complete further education.

## Certification or Licensing

Certification is offered by a number of professional organizations. Requirements typically include graduation from an accredited program, a certain amount of work experience, and passing a written exam. Organizations offering certification include the American Board of Health Physics; the American Board of Industrial Hygiene; the Board of Certified Safety Professionals (BCSP); the Council on Certification of Health, Environmental, and Safety Technologists; and the National Fire Protection Association.

States require licensure for some occupational safety and health workers, depending on the job they do. For example, professional engineers must be licensed, although requirements may vary from state to state. In general, however, requirements include graduation from an accredited program, work experience, and the passing of written exams.

## Other Requirements

You may need to be in good physical condition to keep up with the physical demands of some of the jobs in this field. To be effective in establishing safety programs and procedures, you must be able to communicate well and motivate others. You must be adaptable and able to work comfortably with people on all levels—from union representatives to supervisors of a welding shop to corporate executives or government bureaucrats.

## EXPLORING

Your science teachers, teachers of technical subjects, and school vocational counselors may offer guidance to useful courses of study and any available work-study programs. Math and science clubs may develop your interest in a safety career; debate teams and drama clubs can help you develop communication skills.

You may be able to interview with and attend lectures by occupational safety and health professionals, giving you an opportunity to ask questions and get an overview of the field. Field trips to an industrial plant or other worksite will also give you an appreciation for the profession.

There are no shortcuts in the educational process, but as you begin to fulfill your academic goals, you may seek part-time and summer jobs that are related to your career objectives. These jobs in turn may lead to permanent positions upon graduation. Part-time and summer jobs in manufacturing plants will give you firsthand experience in observing working conditions and help you become familiar with some of the equipment that is important to safety workers. You may also be able to find safety- or health-related jobs in local hospitals and insurance companies. Student internships are a good way to enter the field. One of the best-known internship programs is run by the Department of Occupational and Environmental Safety & Health at the University of Wisconsin–Whitewater (http:// academics.uww.edu/safety).

Another way to study the field is to check out some Web sites, such as those of the Occupational Safety and Health Administration (http://www.osha.gov), Osh.net (http://www.osh.net), and Safety Link (http://www.safetylink.com).

## EMPLOYERS

Occupational health and safety specialists and technicians hold approximately 55,800 jobs and technicians hold 10,900 jobs. Federal, state, and local government agencies employ 41 percent of workers. Major federal employers include the Occupational Safety and Health Administration and the National Institute of Occupational Safety and Health. The remainder work for schools, hospitals, public utilities, scientific and technical consulting firms, mining, quarrying, and oil and gas extraction companies, construction firms, and manufacturing firms.

Occupational safety and health workers are employed throughout the country, but they are generally concentrated in urban and industrial centers. According to the BCSP, the fields of insurance, manufacturing, and chemical production are the largest employers of workers with the CSP designation. Other fields that employ a growing number of professionals with the CSP designation are construction, government, transportation, and aerospace. Many of those employed in the safety and health field are safety engineers, fire protection engineers, industrial hygienists, or workers who combine two or more areas. A small number work as engineering or industrial hygiene technicians. Insurance consultants usually have their offices in one city and travel to and from various sites.

## STARTING OUT

College guidance counselors and career services offices are one source of job leads. People intent on entering the occupational safety and health field may contact the ASSE or other professional societies, talk to company recruiters, or apply directly to the personnel or employment offices of appropriate industrial or insurance companies. Safety-industry trade journals and society Web sites are also excellent sources to check for job listings.

## ADVANCEMENT

Advancement will depend on such factors as a person's education level, area of specialty, experience, and certifications. Safety and health workers in the insurance industry, for example, may be promoted to department manager of a small branch office, then to a larger branch office, and from there to an executive position in the home office. In industrial firms, safety and health workers can move up to safety and health managers for one or more plants. Some working in the consulting area will have the advancement goal of opening their own consulting firm. Safety and health workers who obtain advanced degrees in areas such as public health or safety studies may go into teaching or move into research. Because occupational safety and health workers are so involved with businesses and government, many develop an interest in these fields and add to their credentials by getting a master's in business administration degree or a law degree. They may then go into law, administration, or various aspects of business operations. Technicians with the proper education and experience can advance to professional safety and health positions, with the accompanying increase in prestige and income.

## EARNINGS

Earnings, naturally, vary based on factors such as the field the safety and health worker is involved in, his or her experience, and the size of the employer. Occupational health and safety specialists had median earnings of $63,230 in 2009, according to the U.S. Department of Labor (DOL). The lowest paid 10 percent earned less than $37,910, while the highest paid 10 percent earned more than $93,210. Specialists working for the federal government had mean annual earnings of $76,320 in 2009.

Occupational health and safety technicians earned salaries that ranged from less than $27,080 to $72,300 or more in 2009. Median salaries for these workers were $44,830. Technicians working in electric power generation, transmission and distribution had mean annual earnings of $70,670, while those employed in support activities for mining earned $58,970. Technicians who worked for state governments earned $45,500.

According to the BCSP, salaries for safety workers may range from approximately $30,000 to $150,000 or more. The BCSP also estimates that the average salaries for mid-career professionals with bachelor's or master's degrees range from approximately $60,000 to $75,000. Those with certification typically earn higher salaries.

Those who work full time for one company usually receive health benefits and paid vacation. Consultants and self-employed workers choose their own hours and clients, but they do not usually receive benefits, such as insurance or paid vacation time.

## WORK ENVIRONMENT

Most occupational safety and health workers are based in offices but spend much of their time at worksites, inspecting safety hazards, talking to workers, or taking samples of such things as air, dust, or water. They may travel a great deal, depending on their job specialty and location. For example, safety engineers who work exclusively at one plant may travel only to an occasional seminar or conference, while insurance consultants will spend about half their time away from the office inspecting worksites.

The conditions of inspection sites vary depending on the situation. Safety and health workers may experience unpleasant or dangerous working conditions, such as inspecting mines or livestock-slaughtering procedures. Some factories will be dirty and noisy, while warehouses are usually orderly and office buildings very comfortable. The nature of the work may require a lot of physical activity, such as walking, stooping, bending, and lifting.

# OUTLOOK

According to the DOL, the employment of occupational health and safety specialists and technicians is expected to grow about as fast as the average for all careers through 2018. Because of widespread public support, the economy seldom affects safety jobs (especially government positions), especially in heavy industry where exposure to injury is highest. The expansion of regulatory and compliance programs will increase opportunities in government jobs. In the private sector, employment of safety and health workers is expected to grow because of increasing self-enforcement of government and company regulations. Casualty insurance companies will hire more safety and health workers as small companies request the services of their loss-control and occupational health consultants. Openings will also occur as experienced workers move to other occupations, retire, or are promoted. Employment prospects will be best for college graduates with degrees specifically related to occupational safety or health.

One of the fastest growing areas of safety work is with robotics. The trend toward automation has created a need for safety professionals who can understand electromechanical systems and make sure they meet safety standards. Another growing area is product safety. As more complicated consumer products are marketed to a public that is increasingly aware of safety issues, safety experts will find more opportunities in this field. Other future hotbeds of employment for qualified safety professionals include construction, petrochemicals, the semiconductor industry, multinational corporations, insurance, and meatpacking.

There is an increasing interest among employers in hiring one expert who has knowledge in more than one health and safety specialty, such as health physics, industrial hygiene, and environmental management. Other in-demand specialties include risk management/loss control, ergonomics and human factors engineering, analytical-process safety engineering, construction safety, environmental safety, and fire protection.

# FOR MORE INFORMATION

*For information on certification, visit*
**American Board of Health Physics**
http://www.hps1.org/aahp/boardweb/abhphome.html

*For certification information and industry news, contact*
**American Board of Industrial Hygiene**
6015 West St. Joseph, Suite 102

Lansing, MI 48917-3980
Tel: 517-321-2638
E-mail: abih@abih.org
http://www.abih.org

*For information on the career of industrial hygienist and continuing education, contact*
**American Industrial Hygiene Association**
2700 Prosperity Avenue, Suite 250
Fairfax, VA 22031-4340
Tel: 703-849-8888
E-mail: infonet@aiha.org
http://www.aiha.org

*Visit the society's Web site to read the* Career Guide to the Safety Profession.
**American Society of Safety Engineers**
1800 East Oakton Street
Des Plaines, IL 60018-2100
Tel: 847-699-2929
http://www.asse.org

*For information on certification, contact*
**Board of Certified Safety Professionals**
2301 West Bradley Avenue
Champaign, IL 61821
Tel: 217-359-9263
http://www.bcsp.com

*For information about a career in health physics, contact*
**Health Physics Society**
1313 Dolley Madison Boulevard, Suite 402
McLean, VA 22101-3926
Tel: 703-790-1745
http://www.hps.org

*For certification and education information, contact*
**National Fire Protection Association**
1 Batterymarch Park, PO Box 9101
Quincy, MA 02169-7471
Tel: 800-344-3555
http://www.nfpa.org

*For information on continuing education and safety news, visit the following Web site:*
**National Safety Council**
1121 Spring Lake Drive
Itasca, IL 60143-3201
Tel: 800-621-7615
E-mail: info@nsc.org
http://www.nsc.org

*For information about occupational health and safety, contact*
**Occupational Safety and Health Administration**
U.S. Department of Labor
Office of Communication
200 Constitution Avenue, NW
Washington, DC 20210-0001
Tel: 800-321-6742
http://www.osha.gov

*Visit the society's Web site for information on education and careers.*
**Society of Fire Protection Engineers (SFPE)**
7315 Wisconsin Avenue, Suite 620E
Bethesda, MD 20814-3234
Tel: 301-718-2910
http://www.sfpe.org

*For information on careers in fire protection engineering, visit*
**Fire Protection Engineering**
http://www.careersinfireprotectionengineering.com

# Petroleum Engineers

## QUICK FACTS

**School Subjects**
Mathematics
Physics

**Personal Skills**
Helping/teaching
Technical/scientific

**Work Environment**
Indoors and outdoors
One location with some
travel

**Minimum Education Level**
Bachelor's degree

**Salary Range**
$63,480 to $114,080 to
$158,580+

**Certification or Licensing**
Voluntary (certification)
Required for certain posi-
tions (licensing)

**Outlook**
Faster than the average

**DOT**
010

**GOE**
02.07.04

**NOC**
2145

**O*NET-SOC**
17-2171.00

## OVERVIEW

*Petroleum engineers* apply the principles of geology, physics, and the engineering sciences to the recovery, development, and processing of petroleum. As soon as an exploration team has located an area that could contain oil or gas, petroleum engineers begin their work, which includes determining the best location for drilling new wells, as well as the economic feasibility of developing them. They are also involved in operating oil and gas facilities, monitoring and forecasting reservoir performance, and utilizing enhanced oil recovery techniques that extend the life of wells. There are approximately 21,900 petroleum engineers employed in the United States.

## HISTORY

Within a broad perspective, the history of petroleum engineering can be traced back hundreds of millions of years to when the remains of plants and animals blended with sand and mud and transformed into rock. It is from this ancient underground rock that petroleum is taken, for the organic matter of the plants and animals decomposed into oil during these millions of years and accumulated into pools deep underground.

In primitive times, people did not know how to drill for oil; instead, they collected the liquid substance after it had seeped to above-ground surfaces. Petroleum is known to have been used at that time for caulking ships and for concocting medicines.

Petroleum engineering as we know it today was not established until the mid-1800s, an incredibly long time after the fundamental ingredients of petroleum were deposited within the earth. In 1859, the American Edwin Drake was the first person to ever pump the so-called rock oil from under the ground, an endeavor that, before its success, was laughed at and considered impossible. Forward-thinking investors, however, had believed in the operation and thought that underground oil could be used as inexpensive fluid for lighting lamps and for lubricating machines (and therefore could make them rich). The drilling of the first well, in Titusville, Pennsylvania (1869), ushered in a new worldwide era: the oil age.

At the turn of the century, petroleum was being distilled into kerosene, lubricants, and wax. Gasoline was considered a useless by-product and was run off into rivers as waste. However, this changed with the invention of the internal combustion engine and the automobile. By 1915 there were more than half a million cars in the United States, virtually all of them powered by gasoline.

Edwin Drake's drilling operation struck oil 70 feet below the ground. Since that time, technological advances have been made, and the professional field of petroleum engineering has been established. Today's operations drill as far down as six miles. Because the United States began to rely so much on oil, the country contributed significantly to creating schools and educational programs in this engineering discipline. The world's first petroleum engineering curriculum was devised in the United States in 1914. Today, there are fewer than 30 U.S. and Canadian universities that offer petroleum engineering degrees. The first schools were concerned mainly with developing effective methods of locating oil sites and with devising efficient machinery for drilling wells. Over the years, as sites have been depleted, engineers have been more concerned with formulating methods for extracting as much oil as possible from each well. Today's petroleum engineers focus on issues such as computerized drilling operations; however, because usually only about 40 to 60 percent of each site's oil is extracted, engineers must still deal with designing optimal conditions for maximum oil recovery.

## THE JOB

Petroleum engineer is a rather generalized title that encompasses several specialties, each one playing an important role in ensuring the safe and productive recovery of oil and natural gas. In general, petroleum engineers are involved in the entire process of oil recovery, from preliminary steps, such as analyzing cost factors, to the last stages, such as monitoring the production rate and then repacking the well after it has been depleted.

Petroleum engineering is closely related to the separate engineering discipline of geoscience engineering. Before petroleum engineers can begin work on an oil reservoir, prospective sites must be sought by *geological engineers*, along with *geologists* and *geophysicists*. These scientists determine whether a site has potential oil. Petroleum engineers develop plans for drilling. Drilling is usually unsuccessful, with eight out of 10 test wells being "dusters" (dry wells) and only one of the remaining two test wells having enough oil to be commercially producible. When a significant amount of oil is discovered, engineers can begin their work of maximizing oil production at the site. The development company's *engineering manager* oversees the activities of the various petroleum engineering specialties, including reservoir engineers, drilling engineers, and production engineers.

*Reservoir engineers* use the data gathered by the previous geoscience studies and estimate the actual amount of oil that will be extracted from the reservoir. It is the reservoir engineers who determine whether the oil will be taken by primary methods (simply pumping the oil from the field) or by enhanced methods (using additional energy such as water pressure to force the oil up). The reservoir engineer is responsible for calculating the cost of the recovery process relative to the expected value of the oil produced and simulates future performance using sophisticated computer models. Besides performing studies of existing company-owned oil fields, reservoir engineers also evaluate fields the company is thinking of buying.

*Drilling engineers* work with geologists and drilling contractors to design and supervise drilling operations. They are the engineers involved with the actual drilling of the well. They ask: What will be the best methods for penetrating the earth? It is the responsibility of these workers to supervise the building of the derrick (a platform, constructed over the well, that holds the hoisting devices), choose the equipment, and plan the drilling methods. Drilling engineers must have a thorough understanding of the geological sciences so that they can know, for instance, how much stress to place on the rock being drilled.

*Production engineers* determine the most efficient methods and equipment to optimize oil and gas production. For example, they establish the proper pumping unit configuration and perform tests to determine well fluid levels and pumping load. They plan field workovers and well stimulation techniques such as secondary and tertiary recovery (for example, injecting steam, water, or a special recovery fluid) to maximize field production.

Various research personnel are involved in this field; some are more specialized than others. They include the *research chief engineer,* who directs studies related to the design of new drilling and production methods, the *oil-well equipment research engineer,* who directs research to design improvements in oil-well machinery and devices, and the *oil-field equipment test engineer,* who conducts experiments to determine the effectiveness and safety of these improvements.

In addition to all of the above, sales personnel play an important part in the petroleum industry. *Oil-well equipment and services sales engineers* sell various types of equipment and devices used in all stages of oil recovery. They provide technical support and service to their clients, including oil companies and drilling contractors.

# REQUIREMENTS

## High School
In high school, you can prepare for college engineering programs by taking courses in mathematics, physics, chemistry, geology, and computer science. Economics, history, and English are also highly recommended because these subjects will improve your communication and management skills. Mechanical drawing and foreign languages are also helpful.

## Postsecondary Training
A bachelor's degree in engineering is the minimum requirement. In college, you can follow either a specific petroleum engineering curriculum or a program in a closely related field, such as geophysics or mining engineering. In the United States and Canada, there are fewer than 30 universities and colleges that offer programs that concentrate on petroleum engineering, many of which are located in California and Texas. The first two years toward the bachelor of science degree involve the study of many of the same subjects taken in high school, only at an advanced level, as well as basic engineering courses. In the junior and senior years, students take more specialized courses: geology, formation evaluation, properties of reservoir rocks and fluids, well drilling, properties of reservoir fluids, petroleum production, and reservoir analysis.

Because the technology changes so rapidly, many petroleum engineers continue their education to receive a master's degree and then a doctorate. Petroleum engineers who have earned advanced degrees command higher salaries and often are eligible for better advancement opportunities. Those who work in research and teaching positions are usually required to have these higher credentials.

Students considering an engineering career in the petroleum industry should be aware that the industry employs all kinds of engineers. People with chemical, electrical, geoscience, mechanical, environmental, and other engineering degrees are also employed in this field.

The Society of Petroleum Engineers offers a list of postsecondary petroleum engineering programs at its Web site, http://www.spe.org.

### Certification or Licensing

The Society of Petroleum Engineers offers voluntary certification to petroleum engineers who meet education and experience requirements and pass an examination. Contact the society for more information.

Many jobs, especially public projects, require that the engineer be licensed as a professional engineer. To be licensed, candidates must have a degree from an engineering program accredited by the Accreditation Board for Engineering and Technology. Additional requirements for obtaining the license vary from state to state, but all applicants must take an exam and have several years of related experience on the job or in teaching. For more information on licensing and examination requirements, visit http://www.ncees.org.

### Other Requirements

Students thinking about this career should enjoy science and math. You need to be a creative problem-solver who likes to come up with new ways to get things done and try them out. You need to be curious, wanting to know why and how things are done. You also need to be a logical thinker with a capacity for detail, and you must be a good communicator who can work well with others.

## EXPLORING

One of the most satisfying ways to explore this occupation is to participate in Junior Engineering Technical Society (JETS) programs. JETS participants enter engineering design and problem-solving contests and learn team development skills, often with an engineering mentor. Science fairs and clubs also offer fun and challenging ways to learn about engineering.

Certain students are able to attend summer programs held at colleges and universities that focus on material not traditionally offered in high school. Usually these programs include recreational activities such as basketball, swimming, and track and field. For example, Worcester Polytechnic Institute offers the Frontiers program, a two-week residential session for high school seniors. For more information, visit http://www.wpi.edu/admissions/undergraduate/visit/frontiers.html. The American Indian Science and Engineering

Society (AISES) also sponsors mathematics and science camps that are open to Native American students and held at various college campuses. For more information, visit http://www.aises.org.

Talking with someone who has worked as a petroleum engineer would also be a very helpful and inexpensive way to explore this field. One good way to find an experienced person to talk to is through Internet sites that feature career areas to explore, industry message boards, and mailing lists.

You can also explore this career by touring oilfields or corporate sites (contact the public relations department of oil companies for more information), or you can try to land a temporary or summer job in the petroleum industry on a drilling and production crew. Trade journals, high school counselors, the career services office at technical or community colleges, and the associations listed at the end of this article are other helpful resources that will help you learn more about the career of petroleum engineer.

## EMPLOYERS

Petroleum engineers are employed by major oil companies, as well as smaller oil companies. They work in oil exploration and production. Some petroleum engineers are employed by consulting companies and equipment suppliers. The federal government is also an employer of engineers. In the United States, oil or natural gas is produced in 42 states, with most sites located in California, Louisiana, Oklahoma, and Texas, plus offshore regions. Many other engineers work in other oil-producing areas such as the Arctic Circle, China's Tarim Basin, and the Middle East. Approximately 21,900 petroleum engineers are employed in the United States.

## STARTING OUT

The most common and perhaps the most successful way to obtain a petroleum engineering job is to apply for positions through the career services office at the college you attend. Oil companies often have recruiters who seek potential graduates while they are in their last year of engineering school.

Applicants are also advised to simply check the job sections of major newspapers and apply directly to companies seeking employees. They should also keep informed of the general national employment outlook in this industry by reading trade and association journals, such as the Society of Petroleum Engineers' *Journal of Petroleum Technology* (http://www.spe.org/spe-app/spe/jpt/index.htm).

Engineering internships and co-op programs where students attend classes for a portion of the year and then work in an engineering-related job for the remainder of the year allow students to graduate with valuable work experience sought by employers. Many times these students are employed full time after graduation at the place where they had their internship or co-op job.

As in most engineering professions, entry-level petroleum engineers first work under the supervision of experienced professionals for a number of years. New engineers usually are assigned to a field location where they learn different aspects of field petroleum engineering. Initial responsibilities may include well productivity, reservoir and enhanced recovery studies, production equipment and application design, efficiency analyses, and economic evaluations. Field assignments are followed by other opportunities in regional and headquarters offices.

## ADVANCEMENT

After several years working under professional supervision, engineers can begin to move up to higher levels. Workers often formulate a plan for their advancement during their first years on the job. In the operations division, petroleum engineers can work their way up from the field to district, division, and then operations manager. Some engineers work through various engineering positions from field engineer to staff, then division, and finally chief engineer on a project. Some engineers may advance into top executive management. In any position, however, continued enrollment in educational courses is usually required to keep abreast of technological progress and changes. After about four years of work experience, engineers usually apply for a Professional Engineer license so they can be certified to work on a larger number of projects.

Others earn their master's or doctoral degree so they can advance to more prestigious research engineering, university-level teaching, or consulting positions. Also, petroleum engineers may transfer to many other occupations, such as economics, environmental management, and groundwater hydrology. Finally, some entrepreneurial-minded workers become independent operators and owners of their own oil companies.

## EARNINGS

Petroleum engineers with a bachelor's degree earned average starting salaries of $83,121 in July 2009, according to the National

Association of Colleges and Employers. A survey by the Society of Petroleum Engineers reports the following average salaries in 2009 for members by years of experience: zero to 10 years, $87,600; six to nine years, $121,700; 15 to 19 years, $150,000; and 25 or more years, $186,800.

The U.S. Department of Labor reports that petroleum engineers earned median annual salaries of $114,080 in 2010. Salaries ranged from less than $63,480 to $158,580 or more.

Salary rates tend to reflect the economic health of the petroleum industry as a whole. When the price of oil is high, salaries can be expected to grow; low oil prices often result in stagnant wages.

Fringe benefits for petroleum engineers are good. Most employers provide health and accident insurance, sick pay, retirement plans, profit-sharing plans, and paid vacations. Education benefits are also competitive.

## WORK ENVIRONMENT

Petroleum engineers work all over the world: the high seas, remote jungles, vast deserts, plains, and mountain ranges. Petroleum engineers who are assigned to remote foreign locations may be separated from their families for long periods of time or be required to resettle their families when new job assignments arise. Those working overseas may live in company-supplied housing.

Some petroleum engineers, such as drilling engineers, work primarily out in the field at or near drilling sites in all kinds of weather and environments. The work can be dirty and dangerous. Responsibilities such as making reports, conducting studies of data, and analyzing costs are usually tended to in offices either away from the site or in temporary work trailers.

Other engineers work in offices in cities of varying sizes, with only occasional visits to an oil field. Research engineers work in laboratories much of the time, while those who work as professors spend most of their time on campuses. Workers involved in economics, management, consulting, and government service tend to spend their work time exclusively indoors.

## OUTLOOK

Employment for petroleum engineers is expected to grow faster than the average for all careers through 2018, according to the U.S. Department of Labor. There will be good opportunities for petroleum engineers because the number of degrees granted in petroleum engineering is low, leaving more job openings than there are qualified candidates.

Employment opportunities will become even better if the federal government constructs new gas refineries, pipelines, and transmission lines, as well as drills in areas that were previously off-limits to such development.

Cost-effective technology that permits new drilling and increases production from existing resources will continue to be essential in the profitability of the oil industry. Therefore, petroleum engineers will continue to have a vital role to play, even in this age of streamlined operations and company restructurings.

## FOR MORE INFORMATION

*Visit the association's Web site for information on careers and membership for college students, as well as answers to frequently asked questions about the field.*
American Association of Petroleum Geologists
1444 South Boulder
Tulsa, OK 74119-3604
Tel: 800-364-2274
http://www.aapg.org

*The institute represents the professional interests of oil and natural gas companies. Visit its Web site for career information and facts and statistics about the petroleum industry.*
American Petroleum Institute
1220 L Street, NW
Washington, DC 20005-4070
Tel: 202-682-8000
http://www.api.org

*For information about JETS programs, products, and engineering career brochures (in a variety of disciplines), contact*
Junior Engineering Technical Society (JETS)
1420 King Street, Suite 405
Alexandria, VA 22314-2750
Tel: 703-548-5387
E-mail: info@jets.org
http://www.jets.org

*For a list of petroleum technology schools and information on certification and careers in petroleum engineering, contact*

Society of Petroleum Engineers
222 Palisades Creek Drive
Richardson, TX 75080-2040
Tel: 800-456-6863
E-mail: spedal@spe.org
http://www.spe.org

*For information on career opportunities, scholarships, and mentor programs, contact*
Society of Women Engineers
120 South LaSalle Street, Suite 1515
Chicago, IL 60603-3572
Tel: 877-793-4636
E-mail: hq@swe.org
http://societyofwomenengineers.swe.org

# Petroleum Technicians

## QUICK FACTS

**School Subjects**
Mathematics
Physics

**Personal Skills**
Helping/teaching
Technical/scientific

**Work Environment**
Indoors and outdoors
Primarily multiple locations

**Minimum Education Level**
High school diploma

**Salary Range**
$28,480 to $53,240 to
$96,110+

**Certification or Licensing**
None available

**Outlook**
Little or no change

**DOT**
010

**GOE**
02.05.01

**NOC**
2212

**O*NET-SOC**
19-4041.00, 19-4041.01,
19-4041.0, 47-5011.00,
47-5012.00, 47-5013.00,
47-5021.01

## OVERVIEW

*Petroleum technicians* work in a wide variety of specialties in the petroleum industry. Many kinds of *drilling technicians* drill for petroleum from the earth and beneath the ocean. *Loggers* analyze rock cuttings from drilling and measure characteristics of rock layers. Various types of *production technicians* "complete" wells (prepare wells for production), collect petroleum from producing wells, and control production. *Engineering technicians* help improve drilling technology, maximize field production, and provide technical assistance. *Maintenance technicians* keep machinery and equipment running smoothly. There are approximately 15,200 petroleum and geological technicians employed in the United States.

## HISTORY

In the 1950s and 1960s, the oil industry was relatively stable. Oil was cheap and much in demand. The international oil market was dominated by the "seven sisters"—Shell, Esso, BP, Gulf, Chevron, Texaco, and Mobil. However, by the end of the 1960s, Middle Eastern countries became more dominant. Many nationalized the major oil companies' operations or negotiated to control oil production. To promote and protect their oil production and revenues gained, Iran, Iraq, Kuwait, Saudi Arabia, and Venezuela (a country located in South America) formed OPEC (the Organization of Petroleum Exporting Countries). The Arab producers' policies during the Arab/Israeli War of 1973–74 and the Iranian Revolution in 1978 disrupted oil supplies and skyrocketed oil prices, indicating just how powerful OPEC had become.

By the early 1980s, economic recession and energy conservation measures had resulted in lower oil prices. There was—and still is—worldwide surplus production capacity. OPEC, which expanded membership to countries in the Far East and Africa, tried to impose quotas limiting production, with little success. In 1986, prices—which had once again risen—plummeted.

In the 1990s and 2000s, factors such as strong demand from a growing U.S. population, reductions in domestic oil exploration and production, and conflicts in oil-producing countries such as Iraq caused a significant increase in the price of petroleum.

The events of the 1960s through today have significantly altered the nation's attitude toward the price and availability of petroleum products. The federal government and domestic oil companies have come to realize that foreign sources of oil could easily be lost through regional conflicts or international tensions. To address this crisis, the U.S. government has set a goal of increased domestic production.

These developments have fostered great changes in the technology of oil drilling, in the science related to oil exploration, and in the management of existing oil fields. In many old abandoned fields, scientists found that nearly as much oil remained as had originally been produced from them by older methods. New technology is constantly being developed and used to find ways of extracting more of this remaining oil economically from old and new fields alike.

The career of petroleum technician was created to help the industry meet such challenges. Technological changes require scientifically competent technical workers as crew members for well drilling and oil field management. Well-trained technicians are essential to the oil industry and will continue to be in the future.

# THE JOB

Before petroleum technicians can begin work on an oil reservoir, prospective sites must first be sought out by geological exploration teams. These crews perform seismic surveying, in which sound waves are created and their reflection from underground rocks recorded by seismographs, to help locate potential sources of oil. Other team members collect and examine geological data or test geological samples to determine petroleum and mineral content. They may also use surveying and mapping instruments and techniques to help locate and map test holes or the results of seismic tests.

It is the drill bit, however, that ultimately proves whether or not there is oil. Drilling for oil is a highly skilled operation involving many kinds of technicians: *rotary drillers, derrick operators, engine operators,* and *tool pushers.*

In the most common type of drilling, a drill bit with metal or diamond teeth is suspended on a drilling string consisting of 30-foot pipes joined together. The string is added to as the bit goes deeper. The bit is turned either by a rotary mechanism on the drill floor or, increasingly, by a downhole motor. As drilling progresses, the bit gets worn and has to be replaced. The entire drilling string, sometimes weighing more than 100 tons must be hauled to the surface and dismantled section by section, the bit replaced, then the string reassembled and run back down the well. Known as a "round trip," this operation can take the drilling crew most of a 12-hour shift in a deep well. Until recently, drill strings were mostly manually handled; however, mechanized drill rigs that handle pipe automatically have been introduced to improve safety and efficiency.

The driller directs the crew and is responsible for the machinery operation. The driller watches gauges and works throttles and levers to control the hoisting and rotation speed of the drill pipe and the amount of weight on the bit. Special care is needed as the bit nears oil and gas to avoid a "blow-out." Such "gushers" were common in the early days of the oil industry, but today's drilling technicians are trained to prevent them. Drillers also are responsible for recording the type and depth of strata penetrated each day and materials used.

Derrick operators are next in charge of the drilling crew. They work on a platform high up on the derrick and help handle the upper end of the drilling string during placement and removal. They also mix the special drilling "mud" that is pumped down through the pipe to lubricate and cool the bit as well as help control the flow of oil and gas when oil is struck.

Engine operators run engines to supply power for rotary drilling machinery and oversee their maintenance. They may help when the roughnecks pull or add pipe sections.

Tool pushers are in charge of one or more drilling rigs. They oversee erection of the rig, the selection of drill bits, the operation of drilling machinery, and the mixing of drilling mud. They arrange for the delivery of tools, machinery, fuel, water, and other supplies to the drilling site.

One very specialized drilling position is the *oil-well fishing-tool technician.* These technicians analyze conditions at wells where some object, or "fish," has obstructed the borehole. They direct the work of removing the obstacle (lost equipment or broken drill pipes, for example), choosing from a variety of techniques.

During drilling, *mud test technicians*, also called *mud loggers*, use a microscope at a portable laboratory on-site to analyze drill cuttings carried out of the well by the circulating mud for traces of oil. After final depth is reached, technicians called *well loggers* lower measuring devices to the bottom of the well on cable called wireline. Wireline logs examine the electrical, acoustic, and radioactive properties of the rocks and provide information about rock type and porosity, and how much fluid (oil, gas, or water) it contains. These techniques, known as formation evaluation, help the operating company decide whether enough oil exists to warrant continued drilling.

The first well drilled is an exploration well. If oil is discovered, more wells, called appraisal wells, are drilled to establish the limits of the field. Then the field's economic worth and profit are evaluated. If it is judged economically worthwhile to develop the field, some of the appraisal wells may be used as production wells. The production phase of the operation deals with bringing the well fluids to the surface and preparing them for their trip through the pipeline to the refinery.

The first step is to complete the well—that is, to perform whatever operations are needed to start the well fluids flowing to the surface—and is performed by *well-servicing technicians*. These technicians use a variety of well-completion methods, determined by the oil reservoir's characteristics. Typical tasks include setting and cementing pipe (called production casing) so that the oil can come to the surface without leaking into the upper layers of rock. Well-servicing technicians may later perform maintenance work to improve or maintain the production from a formation already producing oil. These technicians bring in smaller rigs similar to drilling rigs for their work.

After the well has been completed, a structure consisting of control valves, pressure gauges, and chokes (called a Christmas tree because of the way its fittings branch out) is assembled at the top of the well to control the flow of oil and gas. Generally, production crews direct operations for several wells.

Well fluids are often a mixture of oil, gas, and water and must be separated and treated before going into the storage tanks. After separation, *treaters* apply heat, chemicals, electricity, or all three to remove contaminants. They also control well flow when the natural pressure is great enough to force oil from the well without pumping.

*Pumpers* operate, monitor, and maintain production facilities. They visually inspect well equipment to make sure it is functioning properly. They also detect and perform any routine maintenance needs. They adjust pumping cycle time to optimize production and measure the fluid levels in storage tanks, recording the information each day for entry on weekly gauge reports. Pumpers also advise oil haulers or purchasers when a tank is ready for sale.

*Gaugers* ensure that other company personnel and purchasers comply with the company's oil measurement and sale policy. They spotcheck oil measurements and resolve any discrepancies. They also check pumpers' equipment for accuracy and arrange for the replacement of malfunctioning gauging equipment.

Once a field has been brought into production, good reservoir management is needed to ensure that as much oil as possible is recovered. *Production engineering technicians* work with the production engineers to plan field workovers and well stimulation techniques such as secondary and tertiary recovery (for example, injecting steam, water, or a special recovery fluid) to maximize field production. *Reservoir engineering technicians* provide technical assistance to reservoir engineers. They prepare spreadsheets for analyses required for economic evaluations and forecasts. They also gather production data and maintain well histories and decline curves on both company-operated and outside-operated wells.

The petroleum industry has a need for other kinds of technicians as well, including *geological technicians, chemical technicians,* and *civil engineering technicians.*

## REQUIREMENTS

All petroleum technician jobs require at least a high school diploma, and a few specialties require at least a bachelor's degree.

### High School

If you are interested in this field, you should begin preparing in high school by taking algebra, geometry, trigonometry, and calculus classes. Earth science, chemistry, and physics are other useful subjects. High school courses in drafting, mechanics, or auto shop are also valuable preparation, especially for drilling and production technicians. Computer skills are particularly important for engineering technicians, as are typing and English courses.

### Postsecondary Training

As mentioned above, postsecondary training is required for only a few petroleum technician positions. For example, a mud test technician must have at least a bachelor's degree in geology. Although postsecondary training is not usually required for drilling, production, or engineering technicians, these workers can gain familiarity with specified basic processes through special education in technical or community colleges. Postsecondary training can also help entry-level workers compete with experienced workers.

Petroleum technology programs, located primarily at schools in the West and Southwest, are helpful both for newcomers to the field and for those trying to upgrade their job skills. An associate's degree in applied science can be earned by completing a series of technical and education courses.

Petroleum technology programs provide training in drilling operations, fluids, and equipment; production methods; formation evaluation along with the basics of core analysis; and well completion methods and petroleum property evaluation, including evaluation of production history data and basic theories and techniques of economic analysis. These programs emphasize practical applications in the laboratory, field trips, and summer employment, as available.

Specialized training programs designed for oil company employees are offered by the suppliers of special materials, equipment, or services.

## Other Requirements

Petroleum technicians must be able to work with accuracy and precision; mistakes can be costly or hazardous to the technician and to others in the workplace. You should also be able to work both independently and as part of a team, display manual dexterity and mathematical aptitude, and be willing to work irregular hours.

Much of the work in the petroleum industry involves physical labor and is potentially dangerous. Field technicians must be strong and healthy, enjoy the outdoors in all weather, and be flexible and adaptable about working conditions and hours. Drilling crews may be away from their home base for several days at a time, while technicians on offshore rigs must be able to deal with a restricted environment for several days at a time. Petroleum technicians must also like working with machinery, scientific equipment and instruments, and computers. In addition, petroleum technicians must have good eyesight and hearing and excellent hand, eye, and body coordination.

Some technicians must operate off-road vehicles to transport people, supplies, and equipment to drilling and production sites. Most of this task is learned on the job after formal training is completed.

Some petroleum technicians require additional safety training, including hazardous materials training and first-aid training. In some cases, special physical examinations and drug testing are required. Testing and examinations generally take place after technicians are hired.

# EXPLORING

You may want to investigate petroleum technician occupations further by checking your school or public libraries for books on the petroleum industry. Other resources include trade journals, high school counselors, the career services office at technical or community colleges, and the associations and Web sites listed at the end of this article. If you live near an oil field, you may be able to arrange a tour by contacting the public relations department of oil companies or drilling contractors.

Summer and other temporary jobs on drilling and production crews are excellent ways of finding out about this field. Temporary work can provide you with firsthand knowledge of the basics of oil field operations, equipment maintenance, safety, and other aspects of the work. You may also want to consider entering a two-year training program in petroleum technology to learn about the field.

# EMPLOYERS

Although drilling for oil and gas is conducted in 42 states, nearly 75 percent of workers in this field are employed in four states: California, Louisiana, Oklahoma, and Texas. Employers in the crude petroleum and natural gas industry include major oil companies and independent producers. The oil and gas field services industry, which includes drilling contractors, logging companies, and well servicing contractors, is the other major source of employment. Approximately 15,200 petroleum and geological technicians are employed in the United States.

# STARTING OUT

You may enter the field of petroleum drilling or production as a laborer or general helper if you have completed high school. From there, you can work your way up to highly skilled technical jobs, responsibilities, and rewards.

Engineering technicians might start out as *engineering* or *production secretaries* and advance to the position of technician after two to five years of on-the-job experience and demonstrated competency in the use of computers.

Other technicians, such as mud test loggers or well loggers, will need a geology degree first. Upon obtaining your degree, you may start out as an assistant to experienced geologists or petroleum engineers.

Generally speaking, industry recruiters from major companies and employers regularly visit the career services offices of schools with petroleum technology programs and hire technicians before they finish their last year of technical school or college.

Because many graduates have little or no experience with well drilling operations, new technicians work primarily as assistants to the leaders of the operations. They may also help with the semi-skilled or skilled work in order to become familiar with the skills and techniques needed.

It is not uncommon, however, for employers to hire newly graduated technicians and immediately send them to a specialized training program. These programs are designed for oil company employees and usually are offered by the suppliers of the special materials, equipment, or services. After the training period, technicians may be sent anywhere in the world where the company has exploratory drilling or production operations.

## ADVANCEMENT

In oil drilling and production, field advancement comes with experience and on-the-job competency. Although a petroleum technology degree is generally not required, it is clearly helpful in today's competitive climate. On a drilling crew, the usual job progression is as follows: from roughneck or rig builder to derrick operator, rotary driller, to tool pusher, and finally, oil production manager. In production, pumpers and gaugers may later become oil company production foremen or operations foremen; from there, they may proceed to operations management, which oversees an entire district. Managers who begin as technicians gain experience that affords them special skills and judgment.

Self-employment also offers interesting and lucrative opportunities. For example, because many drilling rigs are owned by small, private owners, technicians can become independent owners and operators of drilling rigs. The rewards for successfully operating an independent drill can be very great, especially if the owner discovers new fields and shares in the royalties for production.

Working as a consultant or a technical salesperson can lead to advancement in the petroleum industry. Success is contingent upon an excellent record of field success in oil and gas drilling and production.

In some areas, advancement requires further education. Well loggers who want to analyze logs are required to have at least a bachelor's degree in geology or petroleum engineering, and sometimes they need a master's degree. With additional schooling and a bachelor's degree, an engineering technician can become an engineer. For advanced-level engineering, a master's degree is the minimum requirement and a doctorate is typically required. Upper-level researchers also need a doctorate.

## EARNINGS

Because of their many work situations and conditions, petroleum technicians' salaries vary widely. Salaries also vary according to geographic location, experience, and education. Petroleum and geological technicians had median annual earnings of $53,240 in 2009, according to the U.S. Department of Labor (DOL). Salaries ranged from less than $28,480 to $96,110 or more annually.

In general, technicians working in remote areas and under severe weather conditions usually receive higher rates of pay, as do technicians who work at major oil companies and companies with unions.

Fringe benefits are good. Most employers provide health and accident insurance, sick pay, retirement plans, profit-sharing plans, and paid vacations. Education benefits are also competitive.

## WORK ENVIRONMENT

Petroleum technicians' workplaces and conditions vary as widely as their duties. They may work on land or offshore, at drilling sites or in laboratories, in offices, or refineries.

Field technicians do their work outdoors, day and night, in all kinds of weather. Drilling and production crews work all over the world, often in swamps, deserts, or in the mountains. The work is rugged and physical, and more dangerous than many other kinds of work. Safety is a big concern. Workers are subject to falls and other accidents on rigs, and blowouts can injure or kill workers if well pressure is not controlled.

Drilling crews often move from place to place because work in a particular field may be completed in a few weeks or months. Technicians who work on production wells usually remain in the same location for long periods. Hours are often long for both groups of workers.

Those working on offshore rigs and platforms can experience strong ocean currents, tides, and storms. Living quarters are usually small, like those on a ship, but they are adequate and comfortable. Workers generally live and work on the drilling platform for days at a time and then get several days off away from the rig, returning to shore by helicopter or crew boat.

Engineering technicians generally work indoors in clean, well-lit offices, although some may also spend part of their time in the field. Regular, 40-hour workweeks are the norm, although some may occasionally work irregular hours.

## OUTLOOK

Little or no employment change is expected for petroleum technicians through 2018, according to the DOL. The employment outlook for petroleum technicians is closely linked to the price of oil. When the price of oil is low, companies often reduce exploration and, consequently, the number of technicians needed. When the price of oil is high, more exploration is conducted, and there are more opportunities for technicians.

Besides looking for new fields, companies are also expending much effort to boost production in existing fields. New cost-effective technology that permits new drilling and increases production will continue to be important in helping the profitability of the oil industry.

The oil industry plays an important role in the economy and employment. Oil and gas will continue to be primary energy sources for many decades. Most job openings will be due to retirements and job transfer. Technicians with specialized training will have the best employment opportunities. The DOL reports that professional, scientific, and technical services firms will increasingly seek the services of petroleum technicians who can act as consultants regarding environmental policy and federal pollution mandates.

## FOR MORE INFORMATION

*Visit the association's Web site for information on careers and membership for college students, as well as answers to frequently asked questions about the field.*
American Association of Petroleum Geologists
PO Box 979
Tulsa, OK 74101-0979
Tel: 800-364-2274
http://www.aapg.org

*The institute represents the professional interests of oil and natural gas companies. Visit its Web site for career information and facts and statistics about the petroleum industry.*
American Petroleum Institute
1220 L Street, NW
Washington, DC 20005-4070

Tel: 202-682-8000
http://www.api.org

For information about JETS programs, products, and engineering
career brochures (in many disciplines), contact
Junior Engineering Technical Society (JETS)
1420 King Street, Suite 405
Alexandria, VA 22314-2750
Tel: 703-548-5387
E-mail: info@jets.org
http://www.jets.org

For a list of petroleum technology schools and information on
careers in petroleum engineering, contact
Society of Petroleum Engineers
222 Palisades Creek Drive
Richardson, TX 75080-2040
Tel: 800-456-6863
E-mail: spedal@spe.org
http://www.spe.org

For a training catalog listing publications, audiovisuals, and short
courses, including correspondence courses, contact
University of Texas at Austin
Petroleum Extension Service
2700 W.W. Thorne Boulevard
Houston, TX 77073-3410
Tel: 800-687-4132
http://www.utexas.edu/cee/petex

# Petrologists

## OVERVIEW

*Geologists* study the overall formation of the earth and its history, the movements of the earth's crust, and its mineral compositions and other natural resources. *Petrologists* focus specifically upon the analysis of the composition, structure, and history of rocks and rock formations. Petrologists are also interested in the formation of particular types of rocks that contain economically important materials such as gold, copper, and uranium. They also study the formation and composition of metals, precious stones, minerals, and meteorites, and they analyze a wide variety of substances, ranging from diamonds and gold to petroleum deposits that may be locked in rock formations beneath the earth's surface.

## HISTORY

The field of petrology began to emerge in the early part of the 20th century as a subspecialty within geology. During this period, the mining of oil, coal, precious metals, uranium, and other substances increased rapidly. With the development of the gasoline engine in the mid-1950s, oil became the most significant raw material produced in the world, and the study of the earth's rock formations became invaluable to the mining of petroleum. In fact, the petroleum industry is the largest employer of petrologists; most are employed by one segment or another of the mining industry. Petrologists are also used in many other areas of mining and mineral extraction, and they are employed by numerous government agencies.

# THE JOB

The major goal of petrology is to study the origin, composition, and history of rocks and rock formations. Because petrologists are intimately involved in the mining industry, they may work closely with the following types of scientists: geologists, who study the overall composition and structure of the earth as well as mineral deposits; *geophysicists,* who study the physical movements of the earth including seismic activity and physical properties of the earth and its atmosphere; *hydrologists,* who study the earth's waters and water systems; *mineralogists,* who examine and classify minerals and precious stones; and *paleontologists,* who study the fossilized remains of plants and animals found in geological formations.

Depending upon the type of work they do, petrologists may frequently work in teams with scientists from other specialties. For example, in oil drilling they may work with geologists and geophysicists. The petrologist is responsible for analyzing rocks from bored samples beneath the earth's surface to determine the oil-bearing composition of rock samples as well as to determine whether certain rock formations are likely to have oil or natural gas content. In precious metal mining operations, petrologists may work closely with mineralogists. They may analyze core samples of mineral rock formations, called mineral ore, while the mineralogists analyze in detail the specific mineral or minerals contained in such samples.

Because the surface of the earth is composed of thousands of layers of rock formations shaped over several billion years, the contents of these layers can be revealing, depending upon the rock and mineral composition of each respective layer. Each layer, or stratum, of rock beneath the earth's surface tells a story of the earth's condition in the past and can reveal characteristics such as weather patterns, temperatures, flow of water, movement of glaciers, volcanic activity, and numerous other characteristics. These layers can also reveal the presence of minerals, mineral ores, and extractable fossil fuels such as petroleum and natural gas.

Petrologists spend time both in the field gathering samples and in the laboratory analyzing those samples. They use physical samples, photographs, maps, and diagrams to describe the characteristics of whatever formations they are analyzing. They use chemical compounds to break down rocks and rock materials to isolate certain elements. They use X-rays, spectroscopic examination, electron microscopes, and other sophisticated means of testing and analyzing samples to isolate the specific components of various minerals and elements within the samples in order to draw conclusions from their analyses.

# REQUIREMENTS

## High School

If you are interested in a career in petrology, you should be aware that you will need an extensive education. Begin preparing yourself for this education by taking college prep courses while in high school. It will be important to focus your studies on the sciences, such as earth science, biology, chemistry, and physics, and on mathematics, including algebra, geometry, and calculus. You should also take speech and English classes to hone your research, writing, and speaking skills. In addition, take computer science, geography, and history classes.

## Postsecondary Training

Most professional positions in the field of petrology require a master's degree or a doctorate. Although individuals without these degrees can technically become petrologists, advances in the field and the profession's requirements will make it extremely difficult to enter the field without a graduate degree.

In college, you should concentrate your studies on the earth and physical sciences, geology, paleontology, mineralogy, and, of course, physics, chemistry, and mathematics. Because petrologists frequently analyze large volumes of data and write reports on such data, courses in computer science and English composition are advisable. Many students begin their careers in petrology by first majoring in geology or paleontology as an undergraduate and then, as graduate students, enter formal training in the field of petrology.

The two major professional associations that provide information and continuing education to petrologists are the Geological Society of America and the American Association of Petroleum Geologists. The American Geological Institute GEO Directory (http://www.agiweb.org/workforce/dgd) provides a list of colleges and universities that offer formal training in this area.

## Certification or Licensing

Although no special certification exists for the field of petrology, several states require the registration of petrologists, and government petrologists may be required to take the civil service examination.

## Other Requirements

Requirements for this profession depend in large part upon the segment or subspecialty of the profession you choose. In some cases, petrologists work within a confined geographic area and spend most of their time in laboratories. In other instances, petrologists are called upon to travel throughout the United States and even overseas. Extensive travel is often required if you are working for a multinational oil company or other mining operation where you need to be available on short notice to analyze samples in various localities. Where important mining operations are undertaken, petrologists may be required to analyze rocks, ore, core samples, or other materials on short notice and under deadline pressure.

As with other scientific disciplines, teamwork is often an essential part of the job. Petrologists must be able to understand and relate to geologists, paleontologists, mineralogists, and other scientific experts; they must also be able to relate to and communicate their findings to supervisory personnel who may lack a strong technical background.

If you are considering petrology, you must be able to work well with others, as well as independently, on various projects. You should also enjoy travel and the outdoors.

## EXPLORING

To explore your interest in this field, join your school's science club and any local rock-hunting groups to become actively involved in science. Talk to your science teachers about petrology; they may know of a petrologist you can interview to find out about his or her experiences and education. Your high school counselor may also be able to help you arrange such an information interview. Petrologists may be found in universities and colleges that offer courses in geology and petrology, in certain government offices and field offices, and especially throughout the mining, oil, and natural gas industries.

Both geologists and petrologists require assistance in their work, and it is possible to obtain summer jobs and part-time employment in certain parts of the country where mining or oil exploration activities are taking place. If such work is unavailable to you, try to get a part-time or summer job at a museum in your area that has a geology department, rock collections, or mineral collections. Volunteering at museums is also possible.

For further information about the field of petrology and about various conferences in the geological professions, contact the organizations listed at the end of this article.

## EMPLOYERS

Because much of the practice of petrology relates to the extraction of minerals, fossil fuels, metals, and natural resources, most petrologists work for petroleum and mining companies. Their work includes mining on the earth's surface, beneath the earth's surface, and under the ocean floor (in the case of offshore oil drilling, for example). Other petrologists work for federal, state, and local governments. In the federal branch, petrologists are often employed by the Environmental Protection Agency, the Department of Agriculture, the Department of Energy, the Department of Defense, the Department of Commerce, and the Department of the Interior. In fact, the largest government employer is the U.S. Geological Survey, a branch of the U.S. Department of the Interior. Other petrologists teach earth science in high schools, teach geology and petrology courses in colleges and universities, or work as consultants. In fact, the consulting industry is the most active employer and will probably remain so.

The field of petrology is open to a number of activities and subspecialties, and during their careers petrologists normally specialize in one area.

## STARTING OUT

Both the federal government and state governments employ petrologists in various agencies. Thus, if you are undertaking graduate programs in petrology, you should contact both state civil service agencies in your respective state and the federal Office of Personnel Management (OPM). Federal agencies generally notify the OPM when they wish to fill vacancies in various positions and when new positions are created. The OPM has job information centers located in major cities throughout the United States, as well as a Web site, http://www.usajobs.opm.gov, that lists job openings. You can also obtain job information through employment offices in your state.

Although industrial firms do engage in campus recruiting, particularly for master's- and doctoral-level job applicants, less recruiting is occurring now than in the past. Thus, job seekers should not hesitate to contact oil exploration companies, mining companies, and other organizations directly. It is always a good idea to contact geologists and petrologists directly in various companies to learn about opportunities.

Part-time employment is available to geologists and petrologists in both private industry and various federal and state agencies. In some cases, agencies use volunteer students and scientists and pay only some expenses rather than a full salary. This arrangement may still be a good way to gain experience and to meet professionals in the field.

If you wish to teach petrology, you should consult college and university employment listings. For graduate students in the field, a limited number of part-time jobs, as well as instructor-level jobs, are available.

Note that junior high schools and high schools generally need more instructors in the earth sciences than do colleges. This new reality reflects the fact that many high schools are beginning to offer a broader range of science courses. Individuals with a master's or doctoral degree are likely to be qualified to teach a variety of courses at the high school level, including earth science, physics, chemistry, mathematics, and biology.

## ADVANCEMENT

Because the level of competition in this field is keen and the oil industry is subject to fluctuation, those wishing to enter the petrology profession must think seriously about obtaining the highest level of education possible.

Advancement in the field generally involves spending a number of years as a staff scientist and then taking on supervisory and managerial responsibilities. The abilities to work on a team, to perform accurate and timely research, and to take charge of projects are all important for advancement in this field.

Because petrology, geology, and mineralogy are sciences that overlap, especially in industry, it is possible for petrologists to become mineralogists or geologists under the right circumstances. The fact that the three disciplines are intimately related can work to a person's advantage, particularly in changing economic times.

## EARNINGS

Earnings for petrologists vary according to a person's educational attainment, experience, and ability. A salary survey from the American Association of Petroleum Geologists found that in 2009 petroleum geologists with bachelor's degrees and three to five years of work experience had average salaries of $99,800; with 10–14 years of experience, $110,300; and 25+ years of experience, $189,900. The U.S. Department of Labor (DOL) reports that the median annual salary for geoscientists, except hydrologists and geographers, was $81,220 in 2009. The lowest paid 10 percent earned less than $43,140, while the highest paid 10 percent earned more than $161,260. Geoscientists earned the following mean annual earnings by employer: oil and gas extraction, $136,270; federal government, $94,560; and state government, $62,550.

Petrologists employed by oil companies or consulting firms generally start at somewhat higher salaries than those who work for the government, but private industry favors those with master's or doctoral degrees.

Many petrologists are eligible to receive fringe benefits, such as life and health insurance, paid vacations, and pension plans.

## WORK ENVIRONMENT

Because the field of petrology involves a considerable amount of testing of rocks, ores, and other materials at mining sites and other types of geological sites, petrologists can expect to travel a considerable amount. In some cases, petrologists must travel back and forth from a field site to a laboratory several times while conducting a series of tests. If petrologists are working on exploratory investigations of a potential site for fuel, they may be at a remote location for weeks or months, until the data collected are sufficient to return to the laboratory. The conditions may be arduous, and there may be little to do during leisure time.

The hours and working conditions of petrologists vary, but petrologists working in the field can generally expect long hours. Petrologists, geologists, and mineralogists frequently work in teams, and petrologists may work under the supervision of a head geologist, for example. In private industry, they also frequently work with mining engineers, mine supervisors, drilling supervisors, and others who are all part of a larger mining or drilling operation.

## OUTLOOK

The DOL reports that employment opportunities for geoscientists will grow faster than the average for all occupations through 2018. Opportunities for petrologists—especially those who are employed by the oil and gas industries and consulting firms—will be good. Rising demand for oil throughout the world has spurred an increase in oil drilling and exploration. As a result, the number of new jobs in this field has increased, and the number of students who graduate with degrees in petrology or geology is on the rise. Additionally, environmental regulations will create a need for these scientists in environmental protection and reclamation work. Those with master's degrees, who speak a foreign language, and who are willing to travel abroad for employment will have the best employment prospects.

## FOR MORE INFORMATION

*Visit the association's Web site for information on careers and membership for college students, as well as answers to frequently asked questions about the field.*

American Association of Petroleum Geologists
PO Box 979
Tulsa, OK 74101-0979
Tel: 800-364-2274
http://www.aapg.org

*For information on careers, contact*
American Geological Institute
4220 King Street
Alexandria, VA 22302-1502
Tel: 703-379-2480
http://www.agiweb.org

*For career information, contact*
Association of Environmental and Engineering Geologists
PO Box 460518
Denver, CO 80246-0518
Tel: 303-757-2926
E-mail: aeg@aegweb.org
http://aegweb.org

*For information on internships, contact*
Geological Society of America
PO Box 9140
Boulder, CO 80301-9140
Tel: 888-443-4472
E-mail: gsaservice@geosociety.org
http://www.geosociety.org

*The society is a membership organization for "scientists and engineers involved with coal petrology, kerogen petrology, organic geochemistry and related disciplines." Visit its Web site for more information.*
Society for Organic Petrology
E-mail: info@tsop.org
http://tsop.org

## INTERVIEW

*Dr. Jean Hsieh is a geoscientist at Chevron. She served as president of the Association for Women Geoscientists from 2008 to 2009. She discussed her career with the editors of* Careers in Focus: Energy.

**Q. What is your job title? Where do you work? How long have you worked in the field?**

**A.** My current job title is team leader, carbonate stratigraphy within the Earth Science Department of Chevron's Energy Technology Company. I have worked for Chevron for just over 10 years in Houston, Texas, and in San Ramon, California.

**Q. What made you want to enter this career?**

**A.** I entered this career after starting down the path toward a career in academics. I had finished my Ph.D., did a postdoc, and then started a tenure-track position. Near the end of my postdoc, I started having second thoughts about this career path. Although I enjoyed the research and teaching, I felt that I wanted to do more applied geology and problem solving as I had during my internship in the oil industry. So, I left that career track and started in the oil business. I really enjoy this job because I can take my geological training and my interest in problem solving and apply these to the task of finding and producing oil and gas.

**Q. What is one thing that young people may not know about a career in the geosciences?**

**A.** When I talk to young people, they inevitably say that they enjoy geosciences, but they never thought they could actually get a job doing it. They think that it is a good topic for a "hobby," but not a career. Thus, I think the fact that you can have a job, and a good paying one, in the geosciences is something that they may not know.

**Q. Can you please briefly describe a day in your life on the job?**

**A.** My current job involves being the team leader of a group of "subject matter experts" (i.e., the specialists of the company) for carbonate stratigraphy. My day starts with responding to the numerous e-mails that have come in overnight. Chevron is an international company, and we have offices in almost every time zone. So I often spend several hours responding to technical questions or fielding requests for help on projects. Then, I spend the rest of the day sitting with my employees to talk about their projects. Usually, these are work sessions where we bounce ideas off of one another to come up with the best interpretations. Sometimes we chat about logistics and the best way to plan our projects. Often, there is at least one meeting with my management to keep them up-to-date on the high-priority and high-profile projects.

**Q. What are the most important personal and professional qualities for people in your career?**

**A.** I think the most important personal quality for people in my career is to be open to continual learning. Geosciences are not meant for people who like to know hard facts. There is always a strong sense of probability in our interpretations. Thus, being open to learning new things or ideas is a must. As for professionally, these days, we all work on large teams. Thus, an important quality is communication. Instead of just running around doing a project alone, a geoscientist interacts with a group of other geoscientists, engineers, accounting/financial folks, and planners. The ability to get your message across and thus work well with them is key.

**Q. What do you like most and least about your job?**

**A.** The thing I like most about my job is the interaction I have with my colleagues all day long. The thing I like the least about my job is to provide feedback to my employees that is meant to improve their work (i.e., it is not positive). I think that everyone is always trying hard, but sometimes their energy is misdirected.

**Q. What advice would you give to young people who are interested in the field?**

**A.** My advice would be to try to get internships during the summers when you are not in school. You can check out various industries in the geosciences and pick the one that fits you best. I think you will find that all geoscientists love what they are doing.

**Q. What is the future employment outlook for geoscientists? How is the field changing?**

**A.** I think that future employment is going to be the same or better (meaning a high demand for geoscientists). There is an increasing awareness worldwide about natural resources. We need people to find additional or alternative sources and many people to manage what we have now. The field is changing in that we are able to process data in increasing amounts. Thus, geoscientists need the basics that they are currently learning in school, but also the ability to learn new computing techniques.

# Power Plant Workers

## OVERVIEW

*Power plant workers* include *power plant operators, power distributors,* and *power dispatchers.* In general, power plant operators control the machinery that generates electricity. Power distributors and power dispatchers oversee the flow of electricity through substations and a network of transmission and distribution lines to individual and commercial consumers. The generators in these power plants may produce electricity by converting energy from a nuclear reactor; burning oil, gas, or coal; or harnessing energy from falling water, the sun, or the wind. There are approximately 50,400 power plant workers employed in the United States.

## HISTORY

The first permanent, commercial electric power-generating plant and distribution network was set up in New York City in 1882 under the supervision of the inventor Thomas Edison. Initially, the purpose of the network was to supply electricity to Manhattan buildings equipped with incandescent light bulbs, which had been developed just a few years earlier by Edison. Despite early problems in transmitting power over distance, the demand for electricity grew rapidly. Plant after plant was built to supply communities with electricity, and by 1900 incandescent lighting was a well-established part of urban life. Other uses of electric power were developed as well, and by about 1910 electric power became common in factories, public transportation systems, businesses, and homes.

A power plant operator monitors operations. *(David J. Phillip, AP Photo)*

Many early power plants generated electricity by harnessing water (hydro) power. In hydroelectric plants, which are often located at dams on rivers, giant turbines are turned by falling water, and that energy is converted into electricity. Until the 1930s, hydroelectric plants supplied most electric power because hydro plants were less expensive to operate than plants that relied on thermal energy released by burning fuels such as coal. Afterward, various technological advances made power generation in thermal plants more economical. Burning fossil fuels (coal, oil, or gas) creates heat, which is used to make steam to turn turbines and generate power. During the last several decades, many plants that use nuclear reactors as heat sources for making steam have been in operation.

Today, energy from all these sources—hydropower, burning fossil fuels, and nuclear reactors—is used to generate electricity. Large electric utility systems may generate power from different sources at multiple sites. Although the essentials of generating, distributing, and utilizing electricity have been known for more than a century, the techniques and the equipment have changed. Over the years the equipment used in power generation and distribution has become much more sophisticated, efficient, and centralized, and the use of electric power exceeds the demand for workers.

# THE JOB

Workers in power plants monitor and operate the machinery that generates electric power and sends power out to users in a network of distribution lines. Most employees work for electric utility companies or government agencies that produce power, but there are a small number who work for private companies that make electricity for their own use.

In general, power plant operators who work in plants fueled by coal, oil, or natural gas operate boilers, turbines, generators, and auxiliary equipment such as coal crushers. They also operate switches that control the amount of power created by the various generators and regulate the flow of power to outgoing transmission lines. They keep track of power demands on the system and respond to changes in demand by turning generators on and off and connecting and disconnecting circuits.

Operators must also watch meters and instruments and make frequent tests of the system to check power flow and voltage. They keep records of the load on the generators, power lines, and other equipment in the system, and they record switching operations and any problems or unusual situations that come up during their shifts.

In older plants, *auxiliary equipment operators* work throughout the plant monitoring specific kinds of equipment, such as pumps, fans, compressors, and condensers.

In newer plants, however, these workers have been mostly replaced by automated controls located in a central control room. *Central control room operators* and their assistants work in these nerve centers. Central control rooms are complex installations with many electronic instruments, meters, gauges, switches, as well as software programs, that allow skilled operators to know exactly what is going on with the whole generating system and to quickly pinpoint any trouble that needs repairs or adjustments. In most cases, *mechanics* and *maintenance workers* are the ones who repair the equipment.

The electricity generated in power plants is sent through transmission lines to users at the direction of *load dispatchers*. Load dispatcher workrooms are command posts, where the power generating and distributing activities are coordinated. Pilot boards in the workrooms are like automated maps that display what is going on throughout the entire distribution system. Dispatchers operate converters, transformers, and circuit breakers, based on readings given by monitoring equipment.

By studying factors, such as weather, that affect power use, dispatchers anticipate power needs and tell control room operators how much power will be needed to keep the power supply and demand in balance. If there is a failure in the distribution system, dispatchers redirect the power flow in transmission lines around the problem. They also operate equipment at substations, where the voltage of power in the system is adjusted.

## REQUIREMENTS

### High School
Most employers prefer to hire high school graduates for positions in this occupational field, and often college-level training is desirable. If you are interested in this field, focus on obtaining a solid background in mathematics and science.

### Postsecondary Training
Beginners in this field may start out as helpers or in laborer jobs, or they may begin training for duties in operations, maintenance, or other areas. Those who enter training for operator positions undergo extensive training by their employer, both on the job and in formal classroom settings. The training program is geared toward the particular plant in which they work and usually lasts several years. Even after they are fully qualified as operators or dispatchers, most employees will be required to take continuing education refresher courses. Nuclear power reactor operators often have bachelor's degrees in the physical sciences or engineering.

### Certification or Licensing
Power plants that generate electricity using nuclear reactors are regulated by the Nuclear Regulatory Commission (NRC). Operators in nuclear plants must be licensed by the NRC, because only NRC-licensed operators are authorized to control any equipment in the plant that affects the operation of the nuclear reactor. Nuclear reactor operators are also required to undertake regular drug testing. Power distributors and dispatchers who work in jobs that could affect the power grid must be certified by the North American Energy Reliability Corporation.

### Other Requirements
Key traits for power plant workers include good mathematical and technical skills, the ability to solve problems, attentiveness to detail, and the ability to concentrate for long periods of time.

Although union membership is not necessarily a requirement for employment, many workers in power plants are members of either the International Brotherhood of Electrical Workers or the Utility

Workers Union of America. Union members traditionally are paid better than nonunion members.

## EXPLORING

There is little opportunity for part-time or summer work experience in this field. However, many power plants (both nuclear and nonnuclear) have visitor centers where you can observe some of the power plant operations and learn about the various processes for converting energy into electricity. You might also locate information on this field at libraries, on the Internet, or by contacting the associations listed at the end of this article.

## EMPLOYERS

Employees in the power plant field work in several types of power-generating plants, including those that use natural gas, oil, coal, nuclear, hydro, solar, and wind energies. Because electric utility companies have dominated the energy field, most power plant workers work in electrical utilities. Government agencies that produce power are also employers, as are private companies that make electricity for their own use. Employment opportunities are available in any part of the country, as power plants are scattered nationwide. Approximately 50,400 power plant workers are employed in the United States. About 70 percent of this total are power plant operators, 20 percent are power distributors and dispatchers, and 10 percent are nuclear power reactor operators.

## STARTING OUT

People interested in working in electric power plants can contact local electric utility companies directly. Local offices of utility worker unions may also be sources of information about job opportunities. Leads for specific jobs may be found in newspaper classified ads and through the local offices of the state employment service. Graduates of technical training programs can often get help locating jobs from their schools' career services offices.

## ADVANCEMENT

After they have completed their training, power plant operators may move into supervisory positions, such as the position of shift supervisor. Most opportunities for promotion are within the same plant or at other plants owned by the same utility company. With experience and appropriate training, nuclear power plant operators may advance to become senior reactor operators and shift supervisors.

## EARNINGS

Salaries for workers in the utilities industry are relatively high, but are based on skills and experience, geographical location, union status, and other factors. Operators in conventional (nonnuclear) power plants earned an average salary of $60,400 in 2009, according to the U.S. Department of Labor (DOL). The lowest paid 10 percent of workers earned less than $39,520, while the highest paid 10 percent earned more than $82,770 annually. Power distributors and dispatchers earned a median salary of $66,990 in 2009. Operators in nuclear power plants averaged $72,650 annually in 2009. Salaries ranged from less than $54,590 to $100,310 or more. In many cases, employee salaries are supplemented significantly by overtime pay. Overtime often becomes necessary during power outages and severe weather conditions.

Since power plants operate around the clock, employees work multiple shifts, which can last anywhere from four to 12 hours. In general, workers on night shifts are paid higher salaries than workers on day shifts. In addition to their regular earnings, most workers receive benefits, such as paid vacation days, paid sick leave, health insurance, and pension plans.

## WORK ENVIRONMENT

Most power plants are clean, well lighted, and ventilated. Some areas of the plant may be quite noisy. The work of power plant workers is not physically strenuous; workers usually sit or stand in one place as they perform their duties. Risk of falls, burns, and electric shock increases for those who work outside of the control room. Workers must follow strict safety regulations and sometimes wear protective clothing, such as hard hats and safety shoes, to ensure safety and avoid serious accidents.

Electricity is needed 24 hours a day, every day of the year, so power plants must be staffed at all times. Most workers will work some nights, weekends, and holidays, usually on a rotating basis, so that all employees share the stress and fatigue of working the more difficult shifts.

## OUTLOOK

The DOL predicts little or no employment change for power plant operators through 2018. Power-generating plants are installing more automatic control and computerized systems and more efficient equipment, which is reducing demand for operating staffs. Despite this prediction, the DOL reports that employment opportunities for power plant workers will be excellent because demand for energy is increasing and people will be needed to replace a large number of retiring workers and staff new power plants that are being built.

Jobs in electric power plants are seldom affected by ups and downs in the economy, so employees in the field have rather stable jobs. The DOL reports that workers with "strong technical and mechanical skills and an understanding of science and mathematics" will enjoy the best employment prospects.

## FOR MORE INFORMATION

*For job listings and general information on the power industry, contact*
American Public Power Association
1875 Connecticut Avenue, NW, Suite 1200
Washington, DC 20009-5715
Tel: 800-515-2772
http://www.publicpower.org

*To read* Electricity 101, *visit the institute's Web site.*
Edison Electric Institute
701 Pennsylvania Avenue, NW
Washington, DC 20004-2696
Tel: 202-508-5000
http://www.eei.org

*For information on union membership, contact the following organizations:*
International Brotherhood of Electrical Workers
900 Seventh Street, NW
Washington, DC 20005-3886
Tel: 202-833-7000
http://www.ibew.org

Utility Workers Union of America
815 16th Street, NW
Washington, DC 20006-4101
Tel: 202-974-8200
http://www.uwua.net

*For information on careers and training, visit*
**Get Into Energy**
http://www.getintoenergy.com

*For a fun overview of the energy industry, visit the following Web site:*
**U.S. Energy Information Administration's Kid's Page**
http://www.eia.doe.gov/kids

# Radiation Protection Technicians

## OVERVIEW

Radiation protection technicians, also known as nuclear technicians, monitor radiation levels, protect workers, and decontaminate radioactive areas. They work under the supervision of nuclear scientists, engineers, or power plant managers and are trained in the applications of nuclear and radiation physics to detect, measure, and identify different kinds of nuclear radiation. They know federal regulations and permissible levels of radiation. There are approximately 6,400 radiation protection technicians employed in the United States.

## HISTORY

All forms of energy have the potential to endanger life and property. This potential existed with the most primitive uses of fire, and it exists in the applications of nuclear power. Special care must be taken to prevent uncontrolled radiation in and around nuclear power plants. Skilled nuclear power plant technicians are among the workers who monitor and control radiation levels.

Around 1900, scientists discovered that certain elements give off invisible rays of energy. These elements are said to be radioactive, which means that they emit radiation. Antoine-Henri Becquerel, Marie Curie, and Pierre Curie discovered and described chemical radiation before the turn of the century. In 1910, Marie Curie isolated pure radium, the most radioactive natural element, and in 1911 she was awarded the Nobel Prize for chemistry for her work related to radiation.

Scientists eventually came to understand that radiation has existed in nature since the beginning of time, not only in specific elements on earth, such as uranium, but also in the form of cosmic rays from outer space. All parts of the earth are constantly bombarded by a certain background level of radiation, which is considered normal or tolerable.

During the 20th century, research into the nature of radiation led to many controlled applications of radioactivity, ranging from X-rays to nuclear weapons. One of the most significant of these applications, which has impacted our everyday life, is the use of nuclear fuel to produce energy. Nuclear power reactors produce heat that is used to generate electricity.

Scientists are still trying to completely understand the biological effects of radiation exposure, but we know that short-term effects include nausea, hemorrhaging, and fatigue; long-range and more dangerous effects include cancer, lowered fertility, and possible birth defects. These factors have made it absolutely clear that if radiation energy is to be used for any purpose, the entire process must be controlled. Thus, appropriate methods of radiation protection and monitoring have been developed. The radiation protection technician's job is to ensure that these methods are employed accurately and consistently.

## THE JOB

Radiation protection technicians protect workers, the general public, and the environment from overexposure to radiation. Many of their activities are highly technical in nature: they measure radiation and radioactivity levels in work areas and in the environment by collecting samples of air, water, soil, plants, and other materials; they record test results and inform the appropriate personnel when tests reveal deviations from acceptable levels; they help power plant workers set up equipment that automatically monitors processes within the plant and records deviations from established radiation limits; and they calibrate and maintain such equipment using hand tools.

Radiation protection technicians work efficiently with people of different technical backgrounds. They instruct operations personnel in making the necessary adjustments to correct problems such as excessive radiation levels, discharges of radionuclide materials above acceptable levels, or improper chemical levels. They also prepare reports for supervisory and regulatory agencies.

Radiation protection technicians are concerned with ionizing radiation, particularly three types known by the Greek words *alpha, beta,* and *gamma.* Ionization occurs when atoms split and produce charged particles. If these particles strike the cells in the body, they cause damage by upsetting well-ordered chemical processes.

In addition to understanding the nature and effects of radiation, technicians working in nuclear power plants understand the principles of nuclear power plant systems. They have a thorough knowledge of the instrumentation that is used to monitor radiation in every part of the plant and its immediate surroundings. They also play an important role in educating other workers about radiation monitoring and control.

Radiation protection technicians deal with three basic radiation concepts: time, distance from the radiation source, and shielding. When considering time, technicians know that certain radioactive materials break down into stable elements in a matter of days or even minutes. Other materials, however, continue to emit radioactive particles for thousands of years. Radiation becomes less intense in proportion to its distance from the source, so distance is an important concept in controlling radiation exposure. Shielding is used to protect people from radiation exposure. Appropriate materials with a specific thickness must be used to block emission of radioactive particles.

Because radiation generally cannot be seen, heard, or felt, radiation protection technicians use special instruments to detect and measure it and to determine the extent of radiation exposure. Technicians use devices that measure the ionizing effect of radiation on matter to determine the presence of radiation and, depending on the instrument used, the degree of radiation danger in a given situation.

Two such devices are Geiger counters and dosimeters, which measure received radiation doses. Dosimeters are often in the form of photographic badges worn by personnel and visitors. These badges are able to detect radioactivity because it shows up on photographic film. Radiation protection technicians calculate the amount of time that personnel may work safely in contaminated areas, considering maximum radiation exposure limits and the radiation level in the particular area. They also use specialized equipment to detect and analyze radiation levels and chemical imbalances.

Finally, although the radiation that is released into the environment surrounding a nuclear facility is generally far less than that released through background radiation sources, radiation protection technicians must be prepared to monitor people and environments during abnormal situations and emergencies.

Under normal working conditions, technicians monitor the workforce, the plant, and the nearby environment for radioactive contamination; test plant workers for radiation exposure, both internally and externally; train personnel in the proper use of monitoring and safety equipment; help *nuclear materials handling technicians* prepare and monitor radioactive waste shipments; perform basic radiation orientation training; take radiation contamination and control surveys, air sample surveys, and radiation level surveys; maintain and calibrate radiation detection instruments using standard samples to determine accuracy; ensure that radiation protection regulations, standards, and procedures are followed and records are kept of all regular measurements and radioactivity tests; and carry out decontamination procedures that ensure the safety of plant workers and the continued operation of the plant.

## REQUIREMENTS

### High School

You should have a solid background in basic high school mathematics and science. Take four years of English, at least two years of mathematics including algebra, and at least one year of physical science, preferably physics with laboratory instruction. Computer programming and applications, vocational machine shop operations, and blueprint reading will also provide you with a good foundation for further studies.

### Postsecondary Training

After high school, you will need to study at a two-year technical school or community college. Several public or private technical colleges offer programs designed to prepare nuclear power plant radiation protection technicians. Other programs, called nuclear technology or nuclear materials handling technology, also provide a good foundation. You should be prepared to spend from one to two years in postsecondary technical training taking courses in chemistry, physics, laboratory procedures, and technical writing. Because the job entails accurately recording important data and writing clear, concise technical reports, technicians need excellent writing skills.

A typical first year of study for radiation protection technicians includes introduction to nuclear technology, radiation physics, mathematics, electricity and electronics, technical communications, radiation detection and measurement, inorganic chemistry, radiation protection, blueprint reading, quality assurance/quality control, nuclear systems, computer applications, and radiation biology.

Course work in the second year includes technical writing, advanced radiation protection, applied nuclear chemistry, radiological emergencies, advanced chemistry, radiation shielding, radiation monitoring techniques, advanced radionuclide analysis, occupational safety and health, nuclear systems and safety, radioactive materials disposal and management, and industrial economics.

Students who graduate from nuclear technician programs are usually hired by nuclear power plants and other companies and institutions involved in nuclear-related activities. These employers provide a general orientation to their operations and further training specific to their procedures.

## Certification or Licensing

At present, there are no special requirements for licensing or certification of nuclear power plant radiation protection technicians. Some graduates of radiation control technology programs, however, may want to become nuclear materials handling technicians. For this job, licensing may be required, but the employer usually will arrange for the special study needed to pass the licensing test.

Radiation protection professionals may become registered by completing an examination consisting of 150 multiple-choice questions from the following general categories: applied radiation protection, detection and measurements, and fundamentals. This examination is administered by the National Registry of Radiation Protection Technologists. Professionals who successfully complete this examination are known as registered radiation protection technologists. Registration is not the same as licensing and does not guarantee professional ability, but it can help a technician demonstrate his or her professional competency to prospective employers.

## Other Requirements

The work of a radiation protection technician is very demanding. Technicians must have confidence in their ability to measure and manage potentially dangerous radioactivity on a daily basis. Radiation protection technicians play an important teaching role in the nuclear energy-fueled power plant. They must know the control measures required for every employee and be capable of explaining the reasons for such measures. Because abnormal conditions sometimes develop in the nuclear power industry, technicians must be able to withstand the stress, work long hours without making mistakes, and participate as a cooperating member of a team of experts.

Successful technicians are usually individuals who are able to confidently accept responsibility, communicate effectively in person and on paper, and enjoy doing precise work. Their participation is vital to the successful application of nuclear technology.

Federal security clearances are required for workers in jobs that involve national security. Nuclear Regulatory Commission (NRC) clearance is required for both government and private industry employees in securing related positions. Certain projects may necessitate military clearance with or without NRC clearance. Employers usually help arrange such clearances.

## EXPLORING

Professional associations can provide useful information about radiation and nuclear power. Visit the Web sites of the Nuclear Energy Institute (http://www.nei.org/howitworks) and the American Nuclear Society (http://www.aboutnuclear.org) to learn more about the field.

Ask your school counselor to help you learn more about this occupation. You also can obtain information from the occupational information centers at community and technical colleges.

Your science teacher may be able to arrange field trips and invite speakers to describe various careers. Nuclear reactor facilities are unlikely to provide tours, but they may be able to furnish literature on radiation physics and radiation control. Radiation protection technicians employed at nuclear-related facilities may be invited to speak about their chosen field.

Radiation is used for medical diagnosis and treatment in hospitals all over the country. Radiology departments of local hospitals often provide speakers for science or career classes.

In addition, a utilities company with a nuclear-fired plant may be able to offer you a tour of the visitor's center at the plant, where much interesting and valuable information about nuclear power plant operation is available. Small reactors used for experiments, usually affiliated with universities and research centers, also may give tours.

## EMPLOYERS

Approximately 6,400 radiation protection technicians are employed in the United States. They are employed by government agencies, such as the Department of Energy and the Department of Defense, as well as electric power utilities that operate nuclear plants. Other than utilities (which employ 49 percent of those in the field), technicians are employed by nuclear materials handling and processing facilities, regulatory agencies, nondestructive testing firms, radiopharmaceutical industries, nuclear waste handling facilities, nuclear service firms, and national research laboratories.

# STARTING OUT

The best way to enter this career is to graduate from a radiation control technology program and make use of your school's career services office to find your first job. Another excellent way to enter the career is to join the U.S. Navy and enter its technical training program for various nuclear specialties.

Graduates of radiation control technology programs are usually interviewed and recruited while in school by representatives of companies with nuclear facilities. At that time, they may be hired with arrangements made to begin work soon after graduation. Graduates from strong programs may receive several attractive job offers.

Entry-level jobs for graduate radiation protection technicians include the position of *radiation monitor*. This position involves working in personnel monitoring, decontamination, and area monitoring and reporting. Another entry-level job is *instrument calibration technician*. These technicians test instrument reliability, maintain standard sources, and adjust and calibrate instruments. *Accelerator safety technicians* evaluate nuclear accelerator operating procedures and shielding to ensure personnel safety. *Radiobiology technicians* test the external and internal effects of radiation in plants and animals, collect data on facilities where potential human exposure to radiation exists, and recommend improvements in techniques or facilities.

*Hot-cell operators* conduct experimental design and performance tests involving materials of very high radioactivity. *Environmental survey technicians* gather and prepare radioactive samples from air, water, and food specimens. They may handle nonradioactive test specimens for test comparisons with government standards. *Reactor safety technicians* study personnel safety through the analysis of reactor procedures and shielding and through analysis of radioactivity tests.

# ADVANCEMENT

A variety of positions are available for experienced and well-trained radiation protection technicians. *Research technicians* develop new ideas and techniques in the radiation and nuclear field. *Instrument design technicians* design and prepare specifications and tests for use in advanced radiation instrumentation. *Customer service specialists* work in sales, installation, modification, and maintenance of customers' radiation control equipment. *Radiochemistry technicians* prepare and analyze new and old compounds, utilizing the latest equipment and techniques. *Health physics technicians* train new radiation monitors, analyze existing procedures, and conduct tests of experimental design and radiation safety. *Soils evaluation technicians* assess soil density, radioactivity, and moisture content to determine sources of unusually high levels of radioactivity. *Radioactive waste analysts* develop waste disposal techniques, inventory stored waste, and prepare waste for disposal.

Some of the most attractive opportunities for experienced radiation protection technicians include working as radiation experts for a company or laboratory, or acting as consultants. Consultants may work for nuclear engineering or nuclear industry consulting firms or manage their own consulting businesses.

## EARNINGS

The earnings of radiation protection technicians who are beginning their careers depend on what radiation safety program they work in (nuclear power, federal or state agencies, research laboratories, medical facilities, etc.). They may begin as salaried staff or be paid hourly wages. Technicians who receive hourly wages usually work in shifts and receive premium pay for overtime.

The U.S. Department of Labor reports that annual earnings of nuclear technicians were $67,340 in 2009. Wages ranged from less than $41,330 to more than $92,580.

Earnings are affected by whether technicians remain in their entry-level jobs or become supervisors and whether they become registered radiation protection technologists.

Technicians usually receive benefits, such as paid holidays and vacations, insurance plans, and retirement plans. Because of the rapid changes that occur in the radiation safety industry, many employers pay for job-related study and participation in workshops, seminars, and conferences.

## WORK ENVIRONMENT

Depending on the employer, work environments vary from offices and control rooms to relatively cramped and cold areas of power plants.

Of all power plant employees, radiation protection technicians are perhaps best able to evaluate and protect against the radiation hazards that are an occupational risk of this field. The safety of all plant workers depends on the quality and accuracy of their work.

Radiation protection technicians wear film badges or carry pocket monitors to measure their exposure to radiation. Like all other nuclear power plant employees, technicians wear safety clothing, and radiation-resistant clothing may be required in some areas. This type of clothing contains materials that reduce the level of radiation before it reaches the human body.

In some of the work done by radiation protection technicians, radiation shielding materials, such as lead and concrete, are used to enclose radioactive materials while the technician manipulates these materials from outside the contaminated area. These procedures are called hot-cell operations. In some areas, automatic alarm systems are used to warn of radiation hazards so that proper protection can be maintained.

## OUTLOOK

There are 104 nuclear power plants licensed to operate in the United States. In an effort to offset the effects of rising costs to the public for energy obtained from traditional resources, some government officials are calling for the construction of new nuclear power plants and the relicensing of existing ones. If these plants are constructed and existing plants are relicensed, radiation protection technicians will enjoy increased employment opportunities.

However, even if the nuclear power industry experiences a decline, the employment outlook for radiation protection technicians should remain strong. Technicians are needed to support radiation safety programs in Department of Energy and Department of Defense facilities, hospitals, universities, state regulatory programs, federal regulatory agencies, and many industrial activities. New technicians will be needed to replace retiring technicians or technicians who leave the field for other reasons. Increased efforts to enforce and improve safety and waste management standards may also result in new jobs for technicians. Because radiation programs have been in development for more than half a century, most of the radiation safety programs are well established and rely primarily on technicians to keep them running.

## FOR MORE INFORMATION

*For information on careers, publications, scholarships, and seminars, contact*
American Nuclear Society
555 North Kensington Avenue
LaGrange Park, IL 60526-5535
Tel: 708-352-6611
http://www.ans.org

*This professional organization promotes the practice of radiation safety. For information on the latest issues, radiation facts, and membership, contact*

Health Physics Society
1313 Dolley Madison Boulevard, Suite 402
McLean, VA 22101-3926
Tel: 703-790-1745
http://www.hps.org

*For information on registration, contact*

National Registry of Radiation Protection Technologists
PO Box 3084
Westerly, RI 02891-0936
E-mail: nrrpt@nrrpt.org
http://www.nrrpt.org

*This organization is dedicated to the peaceful use of nuclear technologies. Visit its Web site for career information.*

Nuclear Energy Institute
1776 I Street, NW, Suite 400
Washington, DC 20006-3708
Tel: 202-739-8000
http://www.nei.org

# Renewable Energy Careers

## OVERVIEW

*Renewable energy* is defined as a clean and unlimited source of power or fuel. This energy is harnessed from different sources such as wind, sunlight (solar), water (hydro), organic matter (biomass), and the earth's internal heat (geothermal). Unlike nonrenewable energy sources like oil, natural gas, or coal, or nuclear energy, renewable energy is not based on extracting a limited resource.

The renewable energy industry is actually a vast group of subindustries that offer employment opportunities for people with many different educational backgrounds. *Engineers, scientists, architects, farmers, technicians, operators, mechanics, lawyers, businesspeople, sales workers, human resource and public affairs specialists*, as well as a host of *administrative support workers* make their living by researching, developing, installing, and promoting renewable energy.

Renewable energy accounted for 8.2 percent of total U.S. energy consumption in 2009, according to the U.S. Department of Energy, with about 50 percent being used for the production of electricity.

## HISTORY

Renewable energy resources have been used for centuries. Windmills have long been used to grind grain or pump water. The sun has always been used as

## QUICK FACTS

**School Subjects**
Biology
Chemistry
Mathematics
Physics

**Personal Skills**
Mechanical/manipulative
Technical/scientific

**Work Environment**
Indoors and outdoors (technical positions)
Primarily one location (administrative and support positions)

**Minimum Education Level**
High school diploma (administrative and support positions)
Bachelor's degree (technical and professional positions)

**Salary Range**
$20,000 to $50,000 to $130,000+

**Certification or Licensing**
Recommended for most technical positions (certification)
Required for engineering positions (licensing)
None available (administrative and support positions)

**Outlook**
Faster than the average (wind, solar, and bioenergy industries)
*(continues)*

## QUICK FACTS

**Outlook** *(continued)*
About as fast as the average
(geothermal and hydro-
power industries)

**DOT**
007, 637, 809

**GOE**
02.07.04, 02.08.04

**NOC**
7441

**O*NET-SOC**
11-2011.01, 13-2051.00,
11-3051.03, 11-3051.04,
11-3051.02, 11-3051.06,
11-3051.00, 11-3051.05,
11-3051.01, 11-9012.00,
11-9199.10, 13-1199.01,
13-1199.05, 17-2199.03,
17-2141.01, 17-2199.10,
17-2199.11, 19-2041.01,
19-3011.01, 19-3051.00,
41-3099.01, 47-1011.03,
49-9021.01, 51-8012.00

a source of heat. In 1839, Edmund Becquerel, an early pioneer in solar energy, discovered the photoelectric effect—the production of electricity from sunlight. The power of water that is stored and released from dams has been used for generating electricity. This type of electricity is known as hydropower electricity. Hot springs and underground reservoirs, products of geothermal energy, have long been used as sources of heat. People have burned trees or other organic matter, known as biomass, for warmth or cooking purposes.

However, the early technology of harnessing and producing renewable energy as a source of power or fuel was underdeveloped and expensive. Because of this, the majority of our power needs have been met using nonrenewable resources such as natural gas or fossil fuels. Our use of fossil fuels has caused our nation to rely heavily on foreign sources to meet demand. Our declining national supply of nonrenewable natural resources, coupled by public awareness of the soaring costs and environmental damage caused by the mining, extraction, processing, and use of conventional energy sources, have shed new light on renewable energy sources as a viable solution to our energy needs.

Today, "green" sources of power have earned respect as an important alternative to nonrenewable resources. New research and technology in the past 25 years have enabled self-renewing resources to be harnessed more efficiently and at a lower cost than in the past. The Energy Policy Act of 1992 (which deregulated and restructured the conventional power industries) and the Energy Policy Act of 2005 (which promoted the development of renewable energy resources by offering tax incentives and loan guarantees to the private sector) have presented the public with more choices. Tax incentives at the state and federal level make buying green power more affordable to consumers and for utility companies. Renewable energy sources are used to produce approximately 9.4 percent of all electricity in the United States, according to the U.S. Department of Energy. The

Energy Independence and Security Act of 2007 (which increased the amount of renewable fuels sold in the United States and encouraged the creation of as many as 1.1 million new "green" jobs) has also prompted growth in the renewable energy industry.

# THE JOB

The renewable energy industry can be broken down into the following subindustries: wind, solar, hydropower, geothermal, and bioenergy. A wide variety of career options are available to workers with a high school diploma to advanced degrees. Additionally, many career skills are transferable from one subindustry to another.

## Wind

Wind energy has been the fastest growing energy technology in the world for the past three years, according to the American Wind Energy Association (AWEA). According to the AWEA, the U.S. wind industry contributes directly to the economies of 46 states. In 2009, wind energy made up 9 percent of all renewable energy in the United States, according to the Energy Information Administration (EIA).

The wind turbine is the modern, high-tech equivalent of yesterday's windmill. A single wind turbine can harness the wind's energy to generate enough electricity to power a house or small farm. Wind plants, also called wind farms, are a collection of high-powered turbines that can generate electricity for tens of thousands of homes. In order to achieve this capacity, a variety of technical workers are employed in the wind power industry. Electrical, mechanical, and aeronautical engineers design and test the turbines as well as the wind farms. *Meteorologists* help to identify prime locations for new project sites, and may serve as consultants throughout the duration of a project. Skilled construction workers build the farms; *windsmiths*, sometimes called *mechanical or electrical technicians*, operate and maintain the turbines and other equipment on the farm.

## Solar

In 2009, solar energy made up 1 percent of all renewable energy in the United States, according to the EIA. Its potential as a major energy source is largely untapped.

There are different ways to turn the sun's energy into a useful power source. The most common technology today uses photovoltaic (PV) cells. When a PV cell is directly struck by sunlight, the materials inside it absorb this light. Simply put, the activity of absorption frees electrons, which then travel through a circuit. Electrons traveling

A scientist adjusts a generator on a research turbine. *(Warren Gretz, National Renewable Energy Laboratory)*

through a circuit produce electricity. Many PV cells can be linked together to produce unlimited amounts of electricity.

The Concentrating Solar Power (CSP) technologies use mirrors to focus sunlight onto a receiver. The receiver collects sunlight as heat, which can be used directly, or generated into electricity. The three CSP methods used are parabolic troughs, power towers, and parabolic dishes. Parabolic troughs can produce solar electricity inexpensively compared to the other methods, and can generate enough power for large-scale projects. Power towers can also generate power for large-scale projects, while parabolic dishes are used for smaller scale projects. Using solar collectors and storage tanks, the sun's energy can be used to heat water for swimming pools or buildings. Many schools, hospitals, prisons, and government facilities use solar technology for their water use. A building's design or construction materials can also utilize the sun's energy for its heating and light through passive solar design, water heating, or with electrical PV cells.

Skilled workers are needed for all aspects of solar technology. *Electrical, mechanical, and chemical engineers* work in research and development departments. *Architects*, many of whom specialize in passive solar design and construction, design solar-powered structures. *Technicians, electricians, installers*, and *construction workers* build and maintain solar projects.

## Hydropower

Hydropower is the largest and least expensive type of renewable energy in the United States. In 2009, hydropower energy made up 35 percent of all renewable energy in the United States, according to the EIA.

Hydropower uses the energy of flowing water to produce electricity. Water is retained in a dam or reservoir. When the water is released, it passes through and spins a turbine. The movement of the turbine in turn spins generators, which produces electricity. In "run of the river" projects, dams are not needed. Canals or pipes divert river water to spin turbines.

*Electrical and mechanical engineers and technicians* design, construct, and maintain hydropower projects. *Biologists* and other *environmental scientists* assess the effects of hydropower projects on wildlife and the environment. *Fish farmers* develop fish screens and ladders and other migration-assisting devices. *Recreation managers* and *trail planners* manage and preserve the land surrounding the reservoir or dam.

## Geothermal

In 2009, geothermal energy made up 5 percent of all renewable energy in the United States, according to the EIA.

# Learn More About It

Croston, Glenn. *75 Green Businesses You Can Start to Make Money and Make a Difference*. Newburgh, N.Y.: Entrepreneur Media Inc., 2008.

Llewellyn, A. Bronwyn. *Green Jobs: A Guide to Eco-Friendly Employment*. Cincinnati, Ohio: Adams Media, 2008.

McNamee, Gregory. *Careers in Renewable Energy: Get a Green Energy Job*. Masonville, Colo.: PixyJack Press, 2008.

Renner, Michael, Sean Sweeney, and Jill Kubit. *Green Jobs: Working for People and the Environment*. (Worldwatch Report 177). Washington, D.C.: The Worldwatch Institute, 2008.

Geothermal heat comes from the heat within the earth. Water heated from geothermal energy is tapped from its underground reservoirs and used to heat buildings, grow crops, or melt snow. This direct use of geothermal energy can also be used to generate electricity.

Most water and steam reservoirs are located in the western United States. However, dry rock drilling, a process that drills deeper into the earth's magma, is an innovation that will eventually allow geothermal projects to be undertaken almost anywhere.

Employment opportunities in the geothermal industry are excellent for geologists, *geochemists*, and *geophysicists*, who are needed to research and locate new reservoirs. *Hydraulic engineers, reservoir engineers*, and *drillers* work together to reach and maintain the reservoir's heat supply.

The building of new geothermal projects requires the work of electricians, welders, mechanics, and construction workers. *Drilling workers, machinists*, and *mechanics* also are needed to keep the drilling equipment in good order. *Environmental scientists, chemists*, and other scientists are needed to research and develop new technology to reach other geothermal sources of energy.

## Bioenergy

In 2009, bioenergy made up 50 percent of all renewable energy in the United States, according to the EIA.

Bioenergy is the energy stored in biomass—organic matter such as trees, straw, or corn. Bioenergy can be used directly, as is the case when we burn wood for cooking or heating purposes. Indirect uses include the production of electricity using wood waste or other biomass waste as a source of power. Another important biomass byproduct is ethanol, which is converted from corn. [Note: In the past several years, researchers have found that growing biofuels such as corn in an unsustainable manner can actually be harmful to the environment. Carol Werner, executive director of the Environmental and Energy Study Institute, says that the most environmentally friendly biofuels should be made from agricultural waste products (nonedible food products) and from biomass grown on nonagricultural lands].

*Chemists, biochemists, biologists*, and *agricultural scientists* work together to find faster and less costly ways to produce bioenergy. *Engineers, construction workers, electricians*, and *technicians* build and maintain bioenergy conversion plants. *Farmers* and *foresters* raise and harvest crops or other sources of biomass. *Truck drivers* transport crops to the conversion plants.

## Nontechnical Careers: All Sectors

Within all sectors of the renewable energy industry, nontechnical workers are also needed to perform clerical duties, manage workers, sell, market, and advertise products, maintain records, and educate the public. *Sales and marketing professionals, advertising workers, secretaries, receptionists, customer service representatives, media relations specialists, personnel and human resources specialists, accountants, information technology workers,* and *educators* are just some of the types of nontechnical workers who are employed in this industry.

# REQUIREMENTS

## High School

For many jobs in the renewable energy industry, it pays to have a strong background in science and mathematics. For example, earth science, agriculture, and biology classes will be useful if you plan to work in the hydropower industry researching the effects of a new hydropower project on the surrounding vegetation and animal life. Mathematics, earth science, and chemistry classes will be helpful if you plan to work in the geothermal energy industry identifying and harvesting possible sources of geothermal energy from within the earth. Physics classes will be helpful if you plan to work in the wind industry designing windmills and turbine engines to capture and convert wind energy into electricity, or "green" buildings and homes of the future.

However, you need not be technically gifted in science and math in order to succeed in the renewable energy industry. Computer science classes are useful for workers who use computer-aided design programs, organize research, and maintain basic office records. Finance, accounting, communications, and English classes will be helpful to anyone who is interested in working in the business end of the industry. Taking a foreign language is highly useful since a majority of renewable energy companies are located abroad.

## Postsecondary Training

Most technical jobs in this industry require at least an associate's or bachelor's degree. Courses of study range from environmental science and mathematics to architecture and meteorology. Many people who are employed in the research and development or technical departments of their respective renewable subindustry have bachelor's or master's degrees in electrical, chemical, or mechanical engineering. Some scientists have graduate degrees in engineering or the sciences (such as biology, physics, or chemistry).

A small, but growing, number of colleges offer classes, certificates, and degrees in renewable energy. Visit the following Web sites for lists of programs: http://www1.eere.energy.gov/education/educational_professional.html and http://irecusa.org/irec-programs/workforce-development/education-information/university-courses. A list of wind energy educational programs can be found at http://www.windpoweringamerica.gov.

Four-year degrees in liberal arts, business, or other professional degrees are not required, but are recommended for many nontechnical jobs. For example, a *community affairs representative* or *public relations specialist* should have a communications or journalism background.

### Certification or Licensing

The Association of Energy Engineers offers certification in a variety of specialties. To be considered for certification, a candidate must meet eligibility standards such as a minimum of three years relevant work experience and membership in a professional organization. Most programs consist of classroom work and examination.

Certification and licensing requirements for other jobs in the renewable industry will vary according to the position. Solar panel installers must be certified in order to work on most projects, especially government contracts. Different associations offer certification needs and continuing education training. For example, the Midwest Renewable Energy Association offers certification for those working with photovoltaics. Other organizations that offer certification include the North American Board of Certified Energy Practitioners and the National Institute for Certification in Engineering Technologies.

Contractors in the solar industry must apply for certification to ensure their structures are sound and to industry standards. Contact the industry trade associations for specifics on project certification.

Most states require engineers to be licensed. There are two levels of licensing for engineers. Professional engineers (PEs) have graduated from an accredited engineering curriculum, have four years of engineering experience, and have passed a written exam. Engineering graduates need not wait until they have four years experience, however, to start the licensure process. Those who pass the Fundamentals of Engineering examination after graduating are called engineers in training (EIT) or engineer interns (EI). The EIT certification usually is valid for 10 years. After acquiring suitable work experience, EITs can take the second examination, the Principles and Practice of Engineering exam, to gain full PE licensure. For more information on licensing and examination requirements, visit the National Council of Examiners for Engineering and Surveying's Web site, http://www.ncees.org.

Electricians may require licensure depending on the requirements of their job, as well as the industry sector for which they are employed. All states and the District of Columbia require that architects be licensed before contracting to provide architectural services in that particular state. Though many work in the field without licensure, only licensed architects are required to take legal responsibility for all work.

Truck drivers must meet federal requirements and any requirements established by the state where they are based. All drivers must obtain a state commercial driver's license. Truck drivers involved in interstate commerce must meet requirements of the U.S. Department of Transportation.

## Other Requirements

It's not absolutely necessary to be a technical genius to do well in this industry. "Much of the technical side can be, and is, taught while on the job," says Katy Mattai, director of a regional energy association. "However, it is important to have an interest in environmental issues. If you don't care about saving our environment, or conserving natural resources, maybe you should reconsider this career choice."

Teamwork is important within all sectors of renewable energy. The ability to work with large groups of people, with varying backgrounds and technical knowledge, is a must. Other important traits include strong organizational and communication skills, as well as an interest in continuing to learn throughout one's career.

## EXPLORING

Volunteering is one way to explore the renewable energy industry. Katy Mattai discovered this industry after volunteering at a local energy fair. You can find energy fairs or conventions in your area by contacting energy associations. Your duties may consist of handing out brochures or other simple tasks, but you will have the opportunity to learn about the industry and make contacts.

Many professional associations have student chapters or junior clubs. The National Society of Professional Engineers, for example, has local student chapters specifically designed to help college students learn more about careers in engineering. In addition to providing information about different engineering disciplines, student chapters hold contests and offer information on scholarships and internships.

Industry associations also hold many competitions designed to promote their particular renewable energy sector. You can visit the National Renewable Energy Laboratory's (NREL) Web site (http://www.nrel.gov) for a list of student programs and competitions held throughout the United States. One such contest is the Junior Solar Sprint Car Competitions (http://www.nrel.gov/education/jss_hfc.html) held in Colorado for middle school students. The contest calls for the construction and racing of solar-powered cars. Contestants learn about renewable energy technologies and concepts in a fun, challenging, and exciting setting.

## EMPLOYERS

The renewable energy industry is a large and diverse field. Employment opportunities in each sector exist at manufacturing or research and development companies, both large and small; utilities; government organizations; and nonprofit groups and agencies. Research or education opportunities can be found at universities or trade associations. Because the benefits of renewable energy are a global concern, many employment opportunities can be found outside of the United States.

It is important to note that while employment in the renewable energy industry can be found nationwide, some sectors of the industry tend to be clustered in specific regions of the United States. A good example of this is the wind power industry. Although wind is everywhere, different sections of the United States are windier than other areas. For this reason, wind-related projects tend to be most concentrated in the states of California and Texas, other Western states such as Colorado and New Mexico, the Pacific Northwest (especially Washington), and the Midwest (especially Illinois, Iowa, and Minnesota). Approximately 85,000 people are employed in the wind energy industry, according to the American Wind Energy Association.

There are a wide variety of employment opportunities in solar energy. Contractors, dealers, distributors, builders, utilities, government agencies, manufacturers, installers, and research and development companies can be found throughout the United States. The Southwest has the greatest potential for solar energy, although states such as Washington, New Jersey, New York, and Pennsylvania have also increased their solar energy development. Approximately 60,000 people are employed in the U.S. solar industry, according to the Solar Energy Industries Association.

Currently, most geothermal employment opportunities in the United States exist where most geothermal reservoirs are located—in the Western states (especially California, Nevada, Utah, Hawaii, and Idaho). However, since magma is located everywhere under the earth's surface, better technology and more powerful tools may enable geothermal-related projects to be found throughout the United States. The Geothermal Energy Association estimates that 25,000 people currently work in the geothermal industry.

Hydropower plants are found throughout the United States. Hydropower projects can be separated into two categories: large hydropower projects run by the federal electric utilities and operated by the Bureau of Reclamation and the Army Corps of Engineers, and nonfederal hydropower dams—about 2,600—licensed by the Federal Energy Regulatory Commission. States that rely heavily on hydropower generation of electricity include Washington, California, Oregon, New York, Idaho, Montana, Alabama, Arizona, Tennessee, and Maine.

Biomass is bulky and thus costly to transport. Because of this, bioenergy projects are located where biomass crops are grown. This is a great benefit for many rural areas of the United States since jobs and their economic benefits are kept close to home.

## STARTING OUT

Industry associations are a rich source of information, especially when you are looking for your first job. Association Web sites feature the latest industry news, project developments, market forecasts, and government policies. Professional associations, such as the Association of Energy Engineers, also offer career advice and job postings on their Web sites.

Many companies recruit on campus or at job fairs. Check with your school's career center for upcoming fairs in your area. Other good job hunting resources are trade journals, some of which may have job advertisements in their classifieds sections. Check out notable renewable energy publications and blogs, such as *Solar Industry* (http://www.solarindustrymag.com), *Solar Today* (http://ases.org), and Into the Wind: The AWEA Blog (http://www.aweablog.org).

Internships are also great way to get relevant work experience, not to mention valuable contacts. Many of the larger energy companies and nonprofit groups offer internships (either with pay or for course credit) to junior- or senior-level college students. For example, the NREL offers both undergraduate and graduate students the opportunity to participate in its many research and development programs.

# ADVANCEMENT

Typical advancement paths depend on the type of position. For example, solar panel installers may advance to positions of higher responsibility such as managing other workers. With experience, they may opt to start their own business specializing in panel installation and maintenance. Engineers may start with a position at a small company with local interests and advance to a position of higher responsibility within that same company, for example, director of research and development. Or they may move on to a larger more diverse company such as a public utility, whose interests may cover a broader area.

A nontechnical employee with a background in communications, for example, may advance from the human resource department of a windmill turbine manufacturing company to handle media and communication requests for a state's energy program. With the proper expertise and credentials, he or she may advance to direct a nonprofit organization representing a sector of the renewable energy industry.

# EARNINGS

Very little salary information is available for specific jobs in each subindustry. However, according to the U.S. Department of Labor, the median salary for electrical engineers employed in electric power generation, transmission, and distribution was $84,710 in 2009. Salaries for all electrical engineers ranged from less than $53,510 to more than $126,810.

The Association of Energy Engineers conducted a survey of its members in 2010. It found that they earned an average salary of $96,001. Nearly 10 percent of respondents earned more than $130,000, and nearly 10 percent of respondents earned less than $60,000.

Annual salaries for nontechnical workers vary according to the position, type and size of the employer, and job responsibilities. A typical administrative position would probably pay salaries ranging from $20,000 to $50,000. Those employed by nonprofit organizations tend to earn slightly less than their corporate counterparts. Most employees receive a standard benefits package including medical insurance, paid vacation and sick days, and a retirement savings program.

# WORK ENVIRONMENT

Work environment will vary depending on the industry and the type of position a worker holds. For example, meteorologists in the wind industry may need to travel to distant sites in order to better gauge wind capabilities for a proposed wind turbine project. Solar industry technicians often travel from site to site in order to install or maintain equipment needed for solar projects such as homes, buildings, or thermal generators. Hydropower industry professionals may perform much of their work outdoors. Biologists and fisheries managers work at or near ponds and rivers. Recreation managers may often find themselves developing outdoor walking paths and trails near hydroelectric projects to ensure that vegetation and wildlife are protected. In the geothermal industry, drilling crews work outdoors when they operate heavy drilling tools to locate new reservoirs. Farmers employed by bioenergy companies work outdoors tending their biomass crops. All workers who work outdoors must deal with occasionally extreme weather conditions such as high wind, rain, sleet, snow, and temperature extremes.

Administrative support staff, industry educators, research and development workers, sales and marketing staff, and other nontechnical workers often work indoors in comfortable offices. Many scientists work in laboratories, which are clean, comfortable, and well lit. Most employees work a standard 40-hour week. Important projects or deadlines may require overtime and weekend work.

## OUTLOOK

According to a 2001 National Energy Policy report released by the National Energy Policy Development Group, energy use in the United States increased by 17 percent between 1991 and 2000. However, our energy production increased by a marginal 2.3 percent. Consumption of oil in the United States is projected to increase by 33 percent or more by 2020. Presently, we depend on foreign sources for two out of every three barrels of oil. Natural gas consumption is projected to grow by 50 percent, yet U.S. production will only grow by 14 percent. There is enough coal in the United States to last another 250 years, though that too is limited. Electricity consumption continues to increase faster than conventional methods can produce it, leaving many people and businesses at the mercy of brownouts or blackouts. Political instability in foreign countries, increasing costs, an overreliance on fossil fuels, and growing concern about the effects of the use of fossil fuels on the environment have prompted many to look to renewable energy as a source for unlimited power and fuel.

Overall, prospects are very bright for green-industry jobs. According to the American Solar Energy Society, green industries currently generate 8.5 million jobs in the United States. The society predicts that the industry could grow to provide 40 million jobs by 2030.

The wind industry is the fastest growing sector of the renewable energy industry. The greatest factor in this growth can be attributed to lower production costs. Better technology and equipment have lowered the cost of wind-generated electricity by about 80 percent in the past 20 years; this almost matches the cost of electricity generated by conventional methods such as coal or nuclear. The American Wind Energy Association estimates that the U.S. wind energy industry will triple or even quadruple in the next decade. This is good news for windsmiths, engineers, meteorologists, electricians, and other technical workers.

Solar energy use is already well established in high-value markets such as remote power, satellites, and communications. Industry experts are working to improve current technology and lower costs to bring solar-generated electricity, hot water systems, and solar-optimized buildings to the public. The manufacturing of PV cell systems also presents many employment opportunities. According to the NREL, 67 percent of all PV cell systems are manufactured in the United States. Seventy percent of PV cells manufactured in the United States are exported to other nations, resulting in $300 million in sales every year.

Hydropower is an important renewable energy resource because of its abundance and ability to produce electricity inexpensively without harmful emissions. However, some dams and other water reservoirs have been found to harm fish and wildlife located in or near the project site. The industry has responded to such claims by hiring specialists to protect vegetation and wildlife affected by hydropower projects. Two factors may limit growth in the hydropower industry. First, most potential sites for hydropower projects have already been utilized. Second, the licensing process for hydropower projects is slow and inefficient. License requests must be reviewed and approved by federal and state agencies, which often have a conflict in goals and regulations, making it difficult to obtain a license.

Improved technological advances, such as more powerful drilling tools, have helped the geothermal energy industry grow in the past few years. Employment opportunities are greatest in the West (especially California, Nevada, Utah, Hawaii, Idaho, and Alaska) for the direct use, or drilling, of geothermal energy, and in the Midwest for geothermal heat pumps. However, with advances in technology, employment opportunities will be plentiful throughout the United

States. Long delays in obtaining geothermal land leases from the government could hinder the growth of this industry.

Bioenergy is also experiencing steady growth. Interest in bioenergy will not only stem from its electricity potential, but also the biofuels converted from biomass such as biodiesel, biobutanol, and ethanol). The U.S. Department of Agriculture estimates that 17,000 jobs are created for every million gallons of ethanol, an important biomass byproduct, produced. Employment opportunities will exist for chemists, engineers, and agricultural scientists.

The U.S. Department of Energy reports that advanced water power—such as ocean, river, and tidal currents—is also beginning to be studied as a source of renewable energy. In 2008, the U.S. government set aside approximately $10 million for research and development in the field.

Public interest in renewable energy has grown in the last decade. Research has brought better technology, lowered generating costs, and even developed other uses for renewable energy. However, there are still many barriers that hinder this industry's growth potential including lack of infrastructure to transport renewable energy reliably and competition for local distribution.

## FOR MORE INFORMATION

### Bioenergy
*For industry news and updates and general information on bioenergy, contact*
Renewable Fuels Association
425 Third Street, SW, Suite 1150
Washington, DC 20024-3231
Tel: 202-289-3835
E-mail: info@ethanolrfa.org
http://www.ethanolrfa.org

### General Resources
*Learn more about energy issues and find out about upcoming events and conferences by visiting*
American Council for an Energy-Efficient Economy
529 14th Street, NW, Suite 600
Washington, DC 20045-1000
Tel: 202-507-4000
E-mail: aceeeinfo@aceee.org
http://www.aceee.org

*For information on careers, employment opportunities, certification, membership, and industry surveys, contact*
**Association of Energy Engineers**
4025 Pleasantdale Road, Suite 420
Atlanta, GA 30340-4260
Tel: 770-447-5083
http://www.aeecenter.org

*For general information about the renewable energy industry, contact*
**Energy Efficiency and Renewable Energy**
U.S. Department of Energy
Mail Stop EE-1
Washington, DC 20585
Tel: 877-337-3463
E-mail: eereic@ee.doe.gov
http://www.eere.energy.gov

*For information about renewable energy, contact*
**Interstate Renewable Energy Council**
PO Box 1156
Latham, NY 12110-1156
Tel: 518-458-6059
E-mail: info@irecusa.org
http://irecusa.org

*For information on solar tours, energy fairs, industry workshops, and certification, contact*
**Midwest Renewable Energy Association**
7558 Deer Road
Custer, WI 54423-9734
Tel: 715-592-6595
E-mail: info@midwestrenew.org
https://www.midwestrenew.org

*For more background information on renewable energy, careers, and internships, contact*
**National Renewable Energy Laboratory**
1617 Cole Boulevard
Golden, CO 80401-3305
Tel: 303-275-3000
http://www.nrel.gov

*For information on careers, certification and licensing, membership benefits, or local chapters, contact*
National Society of Professional Engineers
1420 King Street
Alexandria, VA 22314-2794
Tel: 703-684-2800
http://www.nspe.org

*For information on green construction, contact*
U.S. Green Building Council
2101 L Street, NW, Suite 500
Washington, DC 20037-1599
Tel: 800-795-1747
E-mail: info@usgbc.org
http://www.usgbc.org

*For information on careers and training, visit*
Get Into Energy
http://www.getintoenergy.com

## Geothermal
*For general information on the geothermal industry and educational teaching guides, contact*
Geothermal Education Office
664 Hilary Drive
Tiburon, CA 94920-1446
Tel: 415-435-4574
E-mail: geo@marin.org
http://www.geothermal.marin.org

*For industry news and updates, publications, conferences, career opportunities, and membership information, contact*
Geothermal Energy Association
209 Pennsylvania Avenue, SE
Washington, DC 20003-1107
Tel: 202-454-5261
E-mail: research@geo-energy.org
http://www.geo-energy.org

## Hydropower
*For industry news and updates, publications, conferences, and information on careers, contact*

National Hydropower Association
25 Massachusetts Avenue, NW, Suite 450
Washington, DC 20001-7405
Tel: 202-682-1700
E-mail: help@hydro.org
http://www.hydro.org

## Ocean Energy
*For industry information, contact*
Ocean Renewable Energy Coalition
http://www.oceanrenewable.com

## Solar
*For industry news and updates, publications, conferences, career opportunities, and membership information, contact*
American Solar Energy Society
2400 Central Avenue, Suite A
Boulder, CO 80301-2862
Tel: 303-443-3130
E-mail: ases@ases.org
http://www.ases.org

*Visit Solarbuzz's Web site for industry news and job postings.*
Solarbuzz
PO Box 475815
San Francisco, CA 94147-5815
Tel: 888-436-7673
E-mail: contact@solarbuzz.com
http://www.solarbuzz.com

*For industry information, contact*
Solar Electric Power Association
1220 19th Street, NW, Suite 800
Washington, DC 20036-2405
Tel: 202-857-0898
http://www.solarelectricpower.org

*For trade news and updates, publications, conferences, career opportunities, and membership information, contact*
Solar Energy Industries Association
575 7th Street, NW, Suite 400
Washington DC 20004-1612

Tel: 202-682-0556
E-mail: info@seia.org
http://www.seia.org

*Find out about workshops in sustainable living by visiting*
**Solar Living Institute**
PO Box 836
13771 South Highway 101
Hopland, CA 95449-9607
Tel: 707-472-2450
http://www.solarliving.org

## Wind
*For industry news and updates, publications, conferences, career opportunities, and membership information, contact*
**American Wind Energy Association**
1501 M Street, NW, Suite 1000
Washington, DC 20005-1769
Tel: 202-383-2500
E-mail: windmail@awea.org
http://www.awea.org

# Roustabouts

## QUICK FACTS

**School Subjects**
Mathematics
Technical/shop

**Personal Skills**
Mechanical/manipulative
Technical/scientific

**Work Environment**
Primarily outdoors
Primarily multiple locations

**Minimum Education Level**
High school diploma

**Salary Range**
$21,280 to $31,840 to
$51,400+

**Certification or Licensing**
None available

**Outlook**
Decline

**DOT**
869

**GOE**
06.03.01

**NOC**
8615

**O*NET-SOC**
47-5071.00

## OVERVIEW

*Roustabouts* do the routine physical labor and maintenance around oil wells, pipelines, and natural gas facilities. Sample tasks include clearing trees and brush, mixing concrete, manually loading and unloading pipe and other materials onto or from trucks or boats, and assembling pumps, boilers, valves, and steam engines and performing minor repairs on such equipment. Roustabouts find work in about 30 states nationwide, especially Texas, California, Oklahoma, New Mexico, Kansas, Illinois, Kentucky, Wyoming, Colorado, Pennsylvania, and West Virginia. There are approximately 65,700 roustabouts working in the United States.

## HISTORY

In the 19th century, people began to search for oil and extract it from deposits inside the earth. The first exploratory oil well was drilled in 1859 in Titusville, Pennsylvania. After much hard work with crude equipment, the drilling crew struck oil, and within a short time the first oil boom was on.

From the earliest days of drilling for oil, roustabouts have performed the necessary manual labor tasks of clearing the land and preparing the site for drilling. Nowadays, with increasing automation and mechanization in the oil industry, roustabouts routinely operate motorized lifts, power tools, electronic testers, and tablet computers. Although roustabouts still perform such chores as digging trenches or cutting down trees and brush, the advent of labor-saving equipment has enabled roustabouts to assume more maintenance and troubleshooting responsibilities.

# THE JOB

Roustabouts perform a wide range of labor tasks, from picking up trash at well sites to running heavy equipment. Part of their work involves clearing sites that have been selected for drilling and building a solid base for drilling equipment. Roustabouts cut down trees to make way for roads or to reduce fire hazards. They dig trenches for foundations, fill excavated areas, mix up batches of wet concrete, and pour concrete into building forms. Other jobs include loading and unloading pipe and other materials onto or from trucks and boats.

Roustabouts also dig drainage ditches around wells, storage tanks, and other installations. They walk flow lines to locate leaks and clean up spilled oil by bailing it into barrels or other containers. They also paint equipment such as storage tanks and pumping units and clean and repair oil field machinery and equipment.

The tools roustabouts use range from simple hand tools like hammers and shovels to heavy equipment such as backhoes or trackhoes. Roustabouts use heavy wrenches and other hand tools to help break out and replace pipe, valves, and other components for repairs or modifications and truck winches for moving or lifting heavy items. Roustabouts also operate motorized lifts, power tools, and electronic sensors and testers. They also may operate tractors with shredders, forklifts, or ditching machines.

# REQUIREMENTS

## High School

Little or no formal training or experience is required to get a job as a roustabout. However, there are more applicants than there are jobs, which allows employers to be selective, choosing people who have previous experience as a roustabout or formal training in a related area. While in high school, classes in mathematics, shop, and technical training will be helpful in preparing to work as a roustabout.

## Postsecondary Training

More and more applicants have earned an associate's degree in petroleum technology, which demonstrates their familiarity with oil field operations and equipment. In general, any technical training, specialized courses, or pertinent experience can be a definite advantage in securing a job and later in getting promotions to more responsible positions.

## Other Requirements

Roustabouts must be physically fit, with good coordination, agility, and eyesight. They need a current valid vehicle operator's license and

A roustabout takes apart a natural gas drilling rig. *(Jim West, The Image Works)*

a good driving record. Depending on the equipment they operate, roustabouts also may need a commercial driver's license as well as crane and forklift licenses. They must enjoy working outdoors, be willing to work in extreme weather, and often are required to work more than 40 hours a week. In addition, employers may require that job applicants pass a physical examination and a screening test for illegal drug use before hiring them. Applicants also might have to take aptitude tests to determine their mechanical ability.

Roustabouts should be ready to pitch in with extra work when the situation requires it. They should work well both on their own and as part of a crew. Those on offshore platforms must be able to get along with the same people for extended periods of time.

Roustabouts need to be comfortable with an unpredictable field; at times they do not have steady work, and at other times they work several weeks straight with only a few days off. People who become roustabouts often have some unique personal characteristics. Many roustabouts have a taste for challenge, travel, and adventure rather than a settled home life. Others look at the job as a short-term way to gain experience, earn money for college or some other specific expense, or to prepare for a better-paying job in the oil industry.

## EXPLORING

Talking with someone who has worked as a roustabout or in another oil field operations job would be a very helpful and inexpensive way of exploring this field. Those who live near an oil field may be able to arrange a tour by contacting the public relations department of oil companies or drilling contractors. Another option is to drive by oil fields that lie along public roads and public lands and take an unofficial tour by car.

Some summer and other temporary jobs as roustabouts are available, and they provide a good way to find out about this field. Temporary workers can learn firsthand the basics of oil field operations, equipment maintenance, safety, and other aspects of the work. Those individuals who are thinking about this kind of work should also consider entering a two-year training program in petroleum technology to learn about the field.

## EMPLOYERS

Approximately 65,700 roustabouts are employed in the United States. Most roustabouts are employed by oil or gas companies, working with production crews around existing oil or gas facilities. Others work for drilling contractors, which are companies that specialize in drilling new wells. Roustabouts usually work under the supervision of a maintenance superintendent and frequently assist skilled workers such as welders, electricians, and mechanics.

## STARTING OUT

Potential roustabouts can contact drilling contractors or oil companies directly about possible job openings. Information may also be available through the local office of state employment services and online. Graduates of technical training programs may find assistance in locating employment through the career services office at their schools.

Roustabouts usually are hired in the field by the maintenance superintendent or by a local company representative. Many roustabouts learn their skills on the job by working under the supervision of experienced workers. Roustabouts with no previous experience are considered "hands" who learn by helping the lead roustabout and crew. They begin with simple labor jobs, like unloading trucks, and gradually take on more complicated work. As they progress, they learn about oil field operations and equipment, safety practices, and maintenance procedures for the machinery.

To learn the skills they need, some newly hired roustabouts take courses at junior colleges or self-study courses, such as those offered by the University of Texas at Austin (http://www.utexas.edu/ce/petex). Some employers, particularly the major oil companies, help pay for job-related courses that employees take on their own time. Because the turnover rate among roustabouts is fairly high, however, employers are usually reluctant to invest a great deal in specialized training for beginning workers.

## ADVANCEMENT

A job as a roustabout is usually an entry-level position. To advance, roustabouts will need to prove that they can do the work; advancement to a variety of other jobs comes with experience.

Roustabouts who are part of maintenance and operation crews may advance to such positions as switcher, gauger, pumper, or lease operator. Those with proven leadership abilities may eventually become chief operators or maintenance superintendents. Roustabouts who are on drilling crews may advance to become roughnecks, floor hands, or rotary helpers, and, later, derrick operators, drillers, and tool pushers, who are in charge of one or more drilling rigs; they also might become engineering technicians. All of these positions represent a special set of responsibilities in a complex operation. (See Petroleum Technicians for more information.)

Some companies run their own training programs offering employees the opportunity to take specialized courses in welding, electricity, and other craft areas; roustabouts who participate in such courses may be prepared to advance into jobs as welders, electricians, pipefitters, and other craftworkers.

## EARNINGS

The earnings of roustabouts vary depending on the branch of the industry they work in, the region of the country, the hours they work, and other factors. Offshore workers generally earn more than onshore, and roustabouts who work for oil companies generally earn more than those who work for drilling contractors.

The U.S. Department of Labor reports that the median annual salary of roustabouts was $31,840 in 2009. Salaries ranged from less than $21,280 to $51,400 or more annually. Generally, roustabouts receive time and a half for overtime; conversely, employers do not pay them if they finish early during a slow time. Those who work away from home receive additional "sub pay" plus reimbursement for their hotel and other expenses.

Benefits and medical coverage are comparable to other manual laborers.

## WORK ENVIRONMENT

Roustabouts work in and around oil fields, on drilling platforms in oceans, on pipelines that transport oil or gas long distances, and at facilities that capture and distribute natural gas. In onshore oil fields or on ocean platforms, roustabouts work outside in all types of weather. On offshore rigs and platforms, they can experience strong ocean currents, violent storms, and bitterly cold winds. Workers in oil fields onshore may have to contend with extremely hot or cold weather, dust, or insects.

Roustabouts on offshore drilling rigs generally work 12-hour days, seven days a week. After seven days on, they usually get seven days off, although some crews may have to work two to four weeks at a stretch, followed by an equal amount of time off. Workers generally stay on the ocean platform during their whole work shift and return to shore via helicopter or crew boat. It is not unusual for offshore roustabouts to live hundreds of miles from the ocean platform where they work.

In onshore oil fields, roustabouts are more likely to work five-day, 40-hour weeks, although this is not always the case, especially during a "boom." Some roustabouts average between 120 and 130 hours in a two-week pay period. Roustabouts may travel anywhere from a half-mile away to 100 or more miles away to a work site. They take a short lunch and other breaks depending on how busy the crew is. The end of the day might come early in the afternoon or in the middle of the night. Many drilling operations work around the clock until discovering oil or abandoning the location as a dry hole. This requires shifts of workers every day of the week.

Being a roustabout can be stressful due to the long hours and time away from home, family, and friends. Some roustabouts work away from home one to three weeks at a time with only a few days off.

Roustabouts' work is strenuous and potentially dangerous, especially on open-sea drilling platforms. They lift heavy materials and equipment and frequently must bend, stoop, and climb. They have to use caution to avoid falling off derricks and other high places, as well as injuries from being hit by falling objects. They are subject to cuts, scrapes, and sore or strained muscles. Because fire is a hazard around oil operations, roustabouts and other workers must be trained in firefighting and be ready to respond to emergencies.

Roustabouts who work on drilling crews can expect to move from place to place, since drilling at a site may be completed in a few weeks or months. If they are working at a site that is producing oil, they usually remain there for longer periods of time.

## OUTLOOK

The number of roustabout jobs is expected to decline due to continuing advances in oil field automation, changes in production methods, and the overall decline in manufacturing employment.

Despite this prediction, the oil industry still plays an important role in the economy and employment. Oil and gas will continue to be primary energy sources for many years. While few new jobs for roustabouts are expected to develop, they always will be needed, and there will be some openings, as turnover is high among roustabouts, especially in offshore drilling. The work is difficult and dirty enough that many people stay in the job only a short time. The need to replace workers who leave will account for nearly all job openings. Workers who have experience or formal training in the field will have the best chance of being hired.

# FOR MORE INFORMATION

*For facts and statistics about the petroleum industry, contact*
American Petroleum Institute
1220 L Street, NW
Washington, DC 20005-4070
Tel: 202-682-8000
http://www.api.org

*For information on well-servicing careers, contact*
Association of Energy Service Companies
14531 FM 529, Suite 250
Houston, TX 77095-3528
Tel: 713-781-0758
http://www.aesc.net

*For a list of petroleum technology schools, contact*
Society of Petroleum Engineers
222 Palisades Creek Drive
Richardson, TX 75080-2040
Tel: 800-456-6863
E-mail: spedal@spe.org
http://www.spe.org

# Solar Engineers

## QUICK FACTS

**School Subjects**
Computer science
Mathematics
Physics

**Personal Skills**
Mechanical/manipulative
Technical/scientific

**Work Environment**
Indoors and outdoors
Primarily multiple locations

**Minimum Education Level**
Bachelor's degree

**Salary Range**
$49,620 to $95,000 to
$126,810+

**Certification or Licensing**
Required for certain
positions

**Outlook**
About as fast as the average

**DOT**
007, 008, 010, 055, 099

**GOE**
02.07.04

**NOC**
2131, 2132, 2133, 2134,
2145

**O*NET-SOC**
17-2041.00, 17-2051.00,
17-2071.00, 17-2141.00,
17-2171.00, 17-2199.11

## OVERVIEW

*Solar engineers* work in any number of areas of engineering products that help harness energy from the sun. They may research, design, and develop new products, or they may work in testing, production, or maintenance. They may collect and manage data to help design solar systems. Types of products solar engineers work on may include solar panels, solar-powered technology, communications and navigation systems, heating and cooling systems, and even cars.

## HISTORY

People have worshipped the sun and found ways to channel its energy to improve their lives since early times. As far back as 400 B.C., ancient Greeks designed their homes to take advantage of the sun's warmth and light by having the structures face south to capture more heat in the winter. (This is known as "passive solar energy," an old technology that is still used today.) The Romans later improved on these designs by adding more windows to the south side of homes, and by putting glass panes in the windows, which allowed more heat and light into buildings. The Romans were also the first to use glasshouses to grow plants and seeds. And the Greeks and Romans were among the first to use mirrors to reflect the sun's heat to light fires.

Solar cooking is an ancient practice as well, dating at least as far back as the Essenes, an early sect of Jewish people who used the intense desert sun to bake thin grain wafers. In 1767, Swiss naturalist Horace-Bénédict de Saussure created the first solar oven—an insulated, glazed box with a glass-paned cover, which reached temperatures of 190 degrees Fahrenheit. In the 1950s, to aid communities located near deserts, the United Nations (UN) and other agencies funded studies of solar cooking to determine if it was a viable way to reduce reliance on plant life for fuel. The studies proved solar cooking was feasible, and so the UN provided further funding for programs to introduce wooden solar cookers to communities in need, such as in locations where firewood was scarce. Despite the benefits of the cookers, however, most groups ended up sticking with their old cooking methods and turned the cookers into firewood.

Solar cooking is back in force today, though. Solar ovens can now reach temperatures as high as 400 degrees Fahrenheit. Many hobbyists, inventors, and designers have fine-tuned the designs of solar ovens over the years, some turning them into marketable products. And the UN's solar cooking idea has been resurrected. In 2006, the nonprofit organizations Jewish Watch International, KoZon Foundation, and Solar Cookers International successfully launched a program to bring solar cookers to Darfur refugees. Civil war started in 2003 in Darfur (located in Western Sudan, Africa) and violence has raged in the years since. As of 2008, at least 200,000 people had lost their lives and 2.5 million had been displaced. As simple an idea as it seems, solar cookers could actually save lives, because women and girls would no longer need to leave the safety of numbers to head off alone in search of firewood.

## THE JOB

Solar engineering, while an ancient practice, is still a relatively new industry that has caught more mainstream attention only within the past 20 years. With forecasts of fossil fuels' eventual depletion and the focus shifting to sustainable business practices, more engineers are researching and developing solar-powered products as a means to conserve energy.

There are two types of solar energy: *passive solar energy* and *active solar energy*. Passive solar energy, as the name suggests, means that no mechanical devices are needed to gather energy from the sun. Positioning buildings to face the sun is one example of passive solar energy. In direct contrast, mechanical devices are used for active solar energy—to collect, store, and distribute solar energy throughout buildings. For instance, mechanical equipment such as pumps, fans, and blowers are used to gather and distribute solar energy to heat the space inside a home. Active solar energy is just one area in which solar engineers work. They help create active solar-space heating systems that are liquid (e.g., water tanks) or air based (e.g., rock bins that store heat), and active solar-water heating systems that use pumps to circulate and heat fluids.

Solar engineers are frequently electrical, mechanical, civil, chemical, or even petroleum engineers who are working on solar projects and designing photovoltaic systems.

Solar engineers may be responsible for such things as reviewing and assessing solar construction documentation; tracking and monitoring project documentation; evaluating construction issues; meeting with other engineers, developers, and investors to present and review project plans and specifications; participating in industry forums; and possibly even dealing with clients directly. One general requirement for most solar engineering positions is a working knowledge of mechanical and electrical engineering, and an understanding of a range of engineering concepts (such as site assessment, analysis, and design, and energy optimization).

## REQUIREMENTS

### High School
Take classes in math (e.g., algebra, calculus, geometry), science, natural science, communications, and computers. Engineering schools tend to favor students who have taken advanced placement and honors classes, so do your best to pursue course work at this high level.

### Postsecondary Training
There are about 2,900 ABET-accredited (Accreditation Board for Engineering and Technology) programs at more than 600 colleges and universities that offer bachelor's degrees in engineering. Most solar engineers have a bachelor of science in an engineering specialty, such as electrical, civil, mechanical, or chemical engineering. Engineering programs typically include mathematics, physical and life sciences, and computer or laboratory courses. Classes in social sciences or humanities are usually required as well. Many companies prefer to hire engineers with master of science degrees, so those who pursue advanced degrees may have better odds of securing work.

### Certification or Licensing
All 50 states and the District of Columbia require engineers who offer their services to the public to be licensed as professional

engineers (PEs). To be designated as a PE, engineers must have a degree from an engineering program accredited by ABET, four years of relevant work experience, and successfully complete the state examination. For more information on licensing and examination requirements, visit the National Council of Examiners for Engineering and Surveying's Web site, http://www.ncees.org.

## Other Requirements

A passion for solving problems is a key characteristic of all engineers, and particularly of those who work on renewable energy projects. Solar engineers team up with a wide variety of people—from management, fellow engineers, designers, and construction professionals, to developers, clients, investors, and more—so it's essential to have strong communication skills, a flexible attitude, and the ability to get along well with others.

# EXPLORING

Learn more about solar energy by reading magazines such as *Home Power* (http://homepower.com) and *Solar Today* (http://ases.org), and visit Web sites like Build It Solar (http://www.builditsolar.com) to find all sorts of links to solar projects, designs, and experiments that you might even be interested in doing yourself. You can set up a small solar system at home and see firsthand how it works. To get an idea about the types of engineering jobs that are out there, visit such Web sites as Intech.net (http://www.intech.net) and Simply Hired (http://www.simplyhired.com).

# EMPLOYERS

Solar engineering is a growing field. While many engineers are working on solar projects, there are no statistics available yet regarding the number of solar engineers who are working full time. According to the U.S. Department of Labor (DOL), in 2008, there were 278,400 civil engineers, 238,700 mechanical engineers, 157,800 electrical engineers, 31,700 chemical engineers, and 21,900 petroleum engineers employed in the United States.

Power systems companies, solar cell and module manufacturers, solar panel companies, and companies that provide energy-saving services (such as heating and cooling systems, energy audits, etc.) to commercial and residential customers are just a few examples of the types of companies that hire engineers to work on solar projects.

Most engineers, in general, work in architectural, engineering, and related services. Some work for business consulting firms, and manufacturing companies that produce electrical and electronic equipment, business machines, computers and data processing companies, and telecommunications parts. Others work for companies that make automotive electronics, scientific equipment, and aircraft parts; consulting firms; public utilities; and government agencies. Some may also work as private consultants.

## STARTING OUT

See if you can get an internship with a company that provides solar energy services. You can also learn more about the industry by visiting the Web sites of professional associations such as the Institute of Electrical and Electronics Engineers (IEEE), the American Wind Energy Association, and the American Solar Energy Society. If there's an upcoming meeting or event in your area, it may be a good opportunity to meet solar energy professionals, find out about the latest trends, and learn where the job market is heading.

## ADVANCEMENT

Solar engineers who work for companies can advance by taking on more projects, managing more people, and moving up to senior-level positions. They may start their own companies and expand their business by offering more services and opening up branches in other locations. They may also teach at universities and write for various publications.

## EARNINGS

Average annual earnings for solar power engineers were about $95,000 per year in 2011, according to SimplyHired.com. Salaries vary be geographic region. Solar engineers in North Dakota, for example, earned about $79,000 per year, whereas solar engineers in New York City had annual incomes of about $112,000.

Salaries for solar engineers can also vary depending on the type of engineering work they do. According to the U.S. Bureau of Labor Statistics, in 2009 electrical engineers earned annual salaries ranging from $53,510 to $126,810 or more; civil engineers earned slightly lower salaries: $49,620 to $118,320 or more; and mechanical engineers had annual earnings ranging from $49,730 to $117,550 or more.

Benefits for full-time workers include vacation and sick time, health, and sometimes dental, insurance, and pension or 401(k) plans. Self-employed engineers must provide their own benefits.

# WORK ENVIRONMENT

Solar engineers may work indoors or outdoors, depending on the project. Work hours are generally 40 per work, with longer hours required when projects near deadline dates. Solar engineers may work in office buildings, laboratories, or industrial plants. They may spend time outdoors at solar power plants, and may also spend time traveling to different plants and worksites in the United States as well as overseas.

# OUTLOOK

The DOL forecasts that employment for engineers will grow about as fast as the average for all careers through 2018, with little or no employment growth expected for electrical engineers specifically. But engineers working in renewable energy can look forward to better odds of finding work in the years to come, especially as more governments invest money into alternative-energy research and development.

According to Engineering.com, "The solar power market has grown significantly in the past decade," and will continue to do so. Green Living Tips (http://www.greenlivingtips.com) also forecasts growth in the solar industry over the next few years, predicting industry revenue as high as $69.3 billion by 2016—more than four times that of the $15.6 billion solar-power revenue in 2006.

# FOR MORE INFORMATION

*Find solar-power industry news, career information, and listings for events and conferences by visiting the Web sites of these associations.*

American Solar Energy Society
2400 Central Avenue, Suite A
Boulder, CO 80301-2862
Tel: 303-443-3130
E-mail: ases@ases.org
http://www.ases.org

Solar Electric Power Association
1220 19th Street, NW, Suite 401
Washington, DC 20036-2405
Tel: 202-857-0898
http://www.solarelectricpower.org

Solar Energy Industries Association
575 7th Street, NW, Suite 400
Washington, DC 20004-1612
Tel: 202-682-0556
E-mail: info@seia.org
http://www.seia.org

*For information on engineer careers and educational programs,
contact*
Institute of Electrical and Electronics Engineers
2001 L Street, NW, Suite 700
Washington, DC 20036-4910
Tel: 202-785-0017
E-mail: ieeeusa@ieee.org
http://www.ieee.org

*For information about renewable energy, contact*
National Renewable Energy Laboratory
1617 Cole Boulevard
Golden, CO 80401-3305
Tel: 303-275-3000
http://www.nrel.gov

*Visit Solarbuzz's Web site for industry news and job postings.*
Solarbuzz
PO Box 475815
San Francisco, CA 94147-5815
Tel: 888-436-7673
E-mail: contact@solarbuzz.com
http://www.solarbuzz.com

*For information on training, contact*
Solar Living Institute
PO Box 836
13771 South Highway 101
Hopland, CA 95449-9607
Tel: 707-472-2450
http://www.solarliving.org

*For information on careers and training, visit*
Get Into Energy
http://www.getintoenergy.com

# Surveyors

## OVERVIEW

Surveyors mark exact measurements and locations of elevations, points, lines, and contours on or near the earth's surface. They measure distances between points to determine property boundaries and to provide data for mapmaking, construction projects, and other engineering purposes. In addition to working outdoors, surveyors also spend time in offices studying data and writing reports and in courthouses conducting research. There are approximately 147,000 surveyors, cartographers, photogrammetrists, and surveying technicians employed in the United States. Of those, about 57,600 are surveyors and about 12,300 are cartographers and photogrammetrists.

## HISTORY

As the United States expanded from the Atlantic Ocean to the Pacific, people moved over the mountains and plains into the uncharted regions of the West. They found it necessary to chart their routes and to mark property lines and borderlines by surveying and filing claims.

The need for accurate geographical measurements and precise records of those measurements has increased over the years. Surveying measurements are needed to determine the location of a trail, highway, or road; the site of a log cabin, frame house, or skyscraper; the right-of-way for water pipes, drainage ditches, and telephone lines; and for the charting of unexplored regions, bodies of water, land, and underground mines.

As a result, the demand for professional surveyors has grown and become more complex. New computerized systems are now used

**QUICK FACTS**

**School Subjects**
Geography
Mathematics

**Personal Skills**
Communication/ideas
Technical/scientific

**Work Environment**
Primarily outdoors
Primarily multiple locations

**Minimum Education Level**
Some postsecondary training

**Salary Range**
$30,130 to $54,180 to $89,120+

**Certification or Licensing**
Voluntary (certification)
Required (licensing)

**Outlook**
Faster than the average

**DOT**
018

**GOE**
02.08.01

**NOC**
2154

**O*NET-SOC**
17-1022.00

to map, store, and retrieve geographical data more accurately and efficiently. This new technology has not only improved the process of surveying but extended its reach as well. Surveyors can now make detailed maps of ocean floors and the moon's surface.

## THE JOB

It is the surveyor's responsibility to make necessary measurements through an accurate and detailed survey of the area and prepare maps, plots, and reports. The surveyor usually works with a field party consisting of several people. Instrument assistants, called *surveying and mapping technicians*, handle a variety of surveying instruments including the theodolite, transit, steel tapes, level, surveyor's chain, rod, and 3-D laser scanners, lasers, and other electronic equipment. They also use the Global Positioning System (GPS) to take measurements. GPS is a group of satellites above the earth that communicate with receivers on the ground to provide extremely accurate information about the location of the area being measured. In the course of the survey, it is important that all readings be recorded accurately and field notes maintained so that the survey can be checked for accuracy. The *party chief* is a surveyor or surveying and mapping technician who supervises the daily activities of the survey team.

Surveyors may specialize in one or more particular types of surveying.

*Construction surveyors* make surveys for construction projects, such as highways, bridges, airstrips, shopping centers, and housing developments. They establish grades, lines, and other points of reference for construction projects. This survey information is essential to the work of the numerous engineers and the construction crews who build these projects.

*Mine surveyors* make surface and underground surveys, preparing maps of mines and mining operations. Such maps are helpful in examining underground passages within the levels of a mine and assessing the volume and location of raw material available.

*Geophysical prospecting* surveyors locate and mark sites considered likely to contain petroleum deposits. *Oil-well directional surveyors* use sonic, electronic, and nuclear measuring instruments to gauge the presence and amount of oil- and gas-bearing reservoirs. *Pipeline surveyors* determine rights-of-way for oil construction projects, providing information essential to the preparation for and laying of the lines.

*Land surveyors* establish township, property, and other tract-of-land boundary lines. Using maps, notes, or actual land title deeds,

A surveyor conducts a survey for a highway construction project.
*(Bob Daemmrich, The Image Works)*

they survey the land, checking for the accuracy of existing records.
This information is used to prepare legal documents such as deeds
and leases. Land surveyors are also known as *boundary,* or *cadas-
tral, surveyors. Land surveying managers* coordinate the work of

surveyors, their parties, and legal, engineering, architectural, and other staff involved in a project. In addition, these managers develop policy, prepare budgets, certify work upon completion, and handle numerous other administrative duties.

*Geodetic surveyors,* also known as *geodesists,* use satellite observations and other high-accuracy techniques to measure large masses of land, sea, and space that must take into account the curvature of the earth and its geophysical characteristics. Their work is helpful in establishing points of reference for smaller land surveys, determining national boundaries, and preparing maps. *Geodetic computers* calculate latitude, longitude, angles, areas, and other information needed for mapmaking. They work from field notes made by an engineering survey party and also use reference tables and a calculating machine or computer.

*Marine surveyors,* also known as *hydrographic surveyors,* measure harbors, rivers, and other bodies of water. They determine the depth of the water through measuring sound waves in relation to nearby land masses. Their work is essential for planning and constructing navigation projects, such as breakwaters, dams, piers, marinas, and bridges, and for preparing nautical charts and maps.

*Photogrammetric engineers,* also known as *photogrammetrists,* determine the contour of an area to show elevations and depressions and indicate such features as mountains, lakes, rivers, forests, roads, farms, buildings, and other landmarks. Aerial, land, and water photographs are taken with special equipment able to capture images of very large areas. From these pictures, accurate measurements of the terrain and surface features can be made. These surveys are helpful in construction projects and in the preparation of topographical maps. Photogrammetry is particularly helpful in charting areas that are inaccessible or to which travel is difficult.

*Forensic surveyors* serve as expert witnesses in legal proceedings that involve industrial, automobile, or other types of accidents. They gather, analyze, and map data that is used as evidence at a trial, hearing, or lawsuit. These professionals must have extensive experience in the field and be strong communicators in order to explain technical information to people who do not have a background in surveying.

# REQUIREMENTS

## High School

Does this work interest you? If so, you should prepare for it by taking plenty of math and science courses in high school. Take algebra, geometry, and trigonometry to become comfortable making different calculations. Earth science, chemistry, and physics classes will also be helpful. Geography will help you learn about different locations, their characteristics, and cartography. Benefits from taking mechanical drawing and other drafting classes include an increased ability to visualize abstractions, exposure to detailed work, and an understanding of perspectives. Taking computer science classes will prepare you for working with technical surveying equipment.

## Postsecondary Training
You will need a bachelor's degree in surveying to gain employment in this field. Photogrammetrists typically have a bachelor's degree in cartography, geography, surveying, computer science, engineering, forestry, or a physical science.

## Certification or Licensing
The American Congress on Surveying and Mapping (ACSM) has partnered with the Federal Emergency Management Agency to create a certification program for floodplain surveyors. Contact the ACSM for details on the program. The ACSM has also partnered with the Bureau of Land Management to create the certified federal surveyors program. Contact the ACSM for more information.

The American Society for Photogrammetry and Remote Sensing offers voluntary certification for surveyors who specialize in photogrammetry and geographic information systems (GIS). Certification is also provided by the GIS Certification Institute.

All 50 states require that surveyors making property and boundary surveys be licensed or registered. The requirements for licensure vary, but most require a degree in surveying or a related field, a certain number of years of experience, and passing a series of written examinations given by the National Council of Examiners for Engineering and Surveying. Information on specific requirements can be obtained by contacting the licensure department of the state in which you plan to work. If you are seeking employment in the federal government, you must take a civil service examination and meet the educational, experience, and other specified requirements for the position.

## Other Requirements
The ability to work with numbers and perform mathematical computations accurately and quickly is very important. Other helpful qualities are the ability to visualize and understand objects in two and three dimensions (spatial relationships) and the ability to

discriminate between and compare shapes, sizes, lines, shadings, and other forms (form perception).

Surveyors walk a great deal and carry equipment over all types of terrain so endurance and coordination are important physical assets. In addition, surveyors direct and supervise the work of their team, so you should be good at working with other people and demonstrate leadership abilities.

## EXPLORING

While you are in high school, begin to familiarize yourself with terms, projects, and tools used in this profession by reading books and magazines on the topic. One magazine that is available online is *Professional Surveyor Magazine* at http://www.profsurv.com. One of the best opportunities for experience is a summer job with a construction outfit, a mining company, or a company that requires survey work. Even if the job does not involve direct contact with survey crews, it will offer an opportunity to observe surveyors and talk with them about their work.

Some colleges have work-study programs that offer on-the-job experience. These opportunities, like summer or part-time jobs, provide helpful contacts in the field that may lead to future full-time employment. If your college does not offer a work-study program and you can't find a paying summer job, consider volunteering at an appropriate government agency. The U.S. Geological Survey and the Bureau of Land Management usually have volunteer opportunities in select areas.

## EMPLOYERS

Approximately 57,600 surveyors are employed in the United States. About 70 percent of surveying workers in the United States are employed by engineering, architectural, and surveying firms. Federal, state, and local government agencies are the next largest employers of surveying workers. Federal agencies that employ a large number of surveyors include the U.S. Geological Survey, the Bureau of Land Management, the National Oceanic and Atmospheric Administration, the U.S. Forest Service, and the Army Corps of Engineers. The majority of the remaining surveyors work for construction firms, highway departments, oil and gas extraction companies, public utilities, and urban planning and redevelopment agencies. Only a small number of surveyors are self-employed.

# STARTING OUT

Apprentices with a high school education can enter the field as equipment operators or surveying assistants. Those who have postsecondary education can enter the field more easily, beginning as surveying and mapping technicians.

College graduates can learn about job openings through their schools' career services offices or through potential employers that may visit their campus. Many cities have employment agencies that specialize in seeking out workers for positions in surveying and related fields. Check your local newspaper or telephone book to see if such recruiting firms exist in your area.

# ADVANCEMENT

With experience, workers advance through the leadership ranks within a surveying team. Workers begin as assistants and then can move into positions such as senior technician, party chief, and, finally, licensed surveyor. Because surveying work is closely related to other fields, surveyors can move into electrical, mechanical, or chemical engineering or specialize in drafting.

# EARNINGS

Surveyors earned a median annual salary of $54,180 in 2009, according to the U.S. Department of Labor (DOL). The middle 50 percent earned between $39,400 and $72,140 a year. The lowest paid 10 percent earned less than $30,130, and the highest paid 10 percent earned more than $89,120 a year. In general, the federal government paid the highest average wages to its surveyors, $82,110 a year in 2009.

Most positions with the federal, state, and local governments and with private firms provide life and medical insurance, pension, vacation, and holiday benefits.

# WORK ENVIRONMENT

Surveyors work 40-hour weeks except when overtime is necessary to meet a project deadline. The peak work period is during the summer months when weather conditions are most favorable. However, it is not uncommon for the surveyor to be exposed to adverse weather conditions.

Some survey projects may involve hazardous conditions, depending on the region and climate as well as the plant and animal life.

Survey crews may encounter snakes, poison ivy, and other hazardous plant and animal life, and may suffer heat exhaustion, sunburn, and frostbite while in the field. Survey projects, particularly those near construction projects or busy highways, may impose dangers of injury from heavy traffic, flying objects, and other accidental hazards. Unless the surveyor is employed only for office assignments, the work location most likely will change from survey to survey. Some assignments may require the surveyor to be away from home for periods of time.

## OUTLOOK

The DOL predicts that the employment of surveyors will grow faster than the average for all occupations through 2018. The outlook is best for surveyors who have college degrees, advanced field experience, and knowledge of GPS and GIS technology. Growth in urban and suburban areas (with the need for new streets, homes, shopping centers, schools, gas and water lines) will provide employment opportunities. State and federal highway improvement programs and local urban redevelopment programs also will provide jobs for surveyors. The expansion of industrial and business firms and the relocation of some firms to large undeveloped tracts will also create job openings. However, construction projects are closely tied to the state of the economy, so employment may fluctuate from year to year.

## FOR MORE INFORMATION

*For information on geodetic surveying, contact*
**American Association for Geodetic Surveying**
http://www.aagsmo.org

*For information on state affiliates and colleges and universities offering land surveying programs, contact*
**American Congress on Surveying and Mapping**
6 Montgomery Village Avenue, Suite 403
Gaithersburg, MD 20879-3557
Tel: 240-632-9716
http://www.acsm.net

*For information on careers, contact*
**American Society for Photogrammetry and Remote Sensing**
5410 Grosvenor Lane, Suite 210
Bethesda, MD 20814-2160

Tel: 301-493-0290
E-mail: asprs@asprs.org
http://www.asprs.org/career

*For information on volunteer and employment opportunities with
the federal government, contact the following organizations:*
**Bureau of Land Management**
1849 C Street, NW, Room 5665
Washington, DC 20240-0001
Tel: 202-208-3801
http://www.blm.gov

**National Oceanic and Atmospheric Administration**
1401 Constitution Avenue, NW, Room 5128
Washington, DC 20230-0001
http://www.noaa.gov

**U.S. Army Corps of Engineers**
4441 G Street, NW
Washington, DC 20314-1000
Tel: 202-761-0011
http://www.usace.army.mil

**U.S. Environmental Protection Agency**
Ariel Rios Building
1200 Pennsylvania Avenue, NW
Washington, DC 20004-2403
http://www.epa.gov/safewater

**U.S. Forest Service**
**Office of Communication**
1400 Independence Avenue, SW
Mailstop 1111
Washington, DC 20250-1111
E-mail: info@fs.fed.us
http://www.fs.fed.us

**U.S. Geological Survey**
12201 Sunrise Valley Drive
Reston, VA 20192-0002
Tel: 703-648-5953
http://www.usgs.gov

*Visit the society's Web site to read* Cartography and GIS.

**Cartography and Geographic Information Society**
6 Montgomery Village Avenue, Suite 403
Gaithersburg, MD 20879-3557
Tel: 240-632-9716
http://www.cartogis.org

*For more information on certification, contact*
**GIS Certification Institute**
701 Lee Street, Suite 680
Des Plaines, IL 60016-4508
Tel: 847-824-7768
E-mail: info@gisci.org
http://www.gisci.org

*For career information, contact*
**National Society of Professional Surveyors**
6 Montgomery Village Avenue, Suite 403
Gaithersburg, MD 20879-3557
Tel: 240-632-9716
http://www.nspsmo.org

# Index